messy art, full heart

Elaine Davis

Foreword by Shanna Noel

Warner Press, Inc.
Warner Press and Warner Press logo are trademarks of Warner Press, Inc.

Messy Art, Full Heart
Written by Elaine Davis
Artwork and illustrations by Elaine Davis

Copyright ©2021 Elaine Davis
Cover and layout copyright ©2021 Warner Press, Inc.

Scripture quotations are taken from the following:

(ESV)—Scripture quotations marked (ESV) are from the ESV® Bible (The Holy Bible, English Standard Version®), copyright © 2001 by Crossway, a publishing ministry of Good News Publishers. Used by permission. All rights reserved.

(KJV)—Scripture quotations marked (KJV) are taken from the Holy Bible, King James Version. Public domain.

(NIV®)—Scripture quotations marked (NIV®) are taken from the Holy Bible, NEW INTERNATIONAL VERSION®, NIV® Copyright © 1973, 1978, 1984, 2011 by Biblica, Inc.® Used by permission. All rights reserved worldwide.

Images taken from the ESV Journaling Bible® (The Holy Bible, English Standard Version®), copyright 2001 by Crossway, a publishing ministry of Good News Publishers. Used by permission. All rights reserved.

All rights reserved. No part of this publication may be reproduced, stored in a retrieval system, or transmitted in any form or by any means—electronic, mechanical, photocopy, recording, or any other—except for brief quotations in printed reviews, without the prior permission of the publisher.

Requests for information should be sent to:

Warner Press, Inc.
2902 Enterprise Drive
Anderson, IN 46013
www.warnerpress.org

Editors: Julie Campbell, Robin Loisch
Cover by Curtis Corzine
Design and Layout by Karen Muilenburg

ISBN: 9781684343331
Printed in USA

Table of Contents

Dedication

For Quinn. May you never lose that childlike faith in the Lord
and always keep a creative spirit.

And for Ian for always inspiring me to be better.

Foreword

I will never forget when I first met Elaine! I was teaching a workshop in her home state, and I was immediately curious about her art. You could tell she had a passion for documenting her faith story in a unique way, and I was totally drawn in from the moment I met her. Her attention to detail while creating unique ways to tell a story is still drawing me in over five years later.

One of the things I love most about this book is that Elaine invites you along for the journey every step of the way. She isn't afraid to share the most intimate details of what God has done in her life, and she encourages you to tell yours as well. Elaine will not only inspire you to document your testimony, but she will also teach you some amazingly fun art techniques along the way.

Over the past several years, I have seen and even written many books on Bible journaling. But what I love about Elaine's book is that it provides the perfect combination of artistic expression and instruction. Art is paired with the devotional content, all while pointing you right back to the most important book of all, the Bible. So if you are brand new to Bible journaling or have been marking up your Bible with notes and highlighters for many years, I promise you that Elaine has something JUST for you in this book, and it will be one that you bookmark and go back to time and time again!

So friends, what are you waiting for? Grab your Bible and get your paint-brushes ready as you head off on a journey with your new best friend, Elaine!

—*Shanna Noel*
Owner of Illustrated Faith
and author of *100 Days of Prayer*

How to Use This Book

Pace and Schedule

Alrighty, friend—*Messy Art, Full Heart* was designed with an easy-to-use format that's versatile for all different types of small groups and independent studies! You can work through it as slowly or as quickly as you like! The book is split up into four weeks, and each week is divided into five days. This gives you twenty sessions to work through alone or with a group. You can stick to the provided schedule of a four-week study, or you can work through one day of the study each week of your small group. Whatever works best for you is the perfect pace!

Creative Component

At the end of every day, you'll find a section called "Creative Heart Check" with prompts to jump start your creative juices. These prompts encourage you to respond creatively to each day of the study. You can use them to inspire your creative direction for each Bible journaling entry. Some of you might be thinking, "What if I don't have a journaling Bible?" The answer to that is, "Never fear!" There are no rules to creativity! You can get artsy in whatever format or medium speaks to you. You can do your creative entries in a journaling Bible, an art journal, a notebook, or even a creative planner. Throughout the book, you'll see some examples of different ways I like to work, including in a Bible, an art journal, and even creating collage tags!

Leader's Guide

The Leader's Guide included in the book is a fabulous resource that will provide you with discussion topics, additional scriptures, and even creative demos you can do with your group! It also includes a sample class schedule and supply list you can adapt to fit your own needs. On the flip side, you don't have to be a leader to benefit from the Leader's Guide. You can use the Book Outline and Companion Material (p. 72) as additional thought-provoking prompts and creative challenges for you to explore on your own. Go for it!

Introduction

Hiya sweets! I'm overjoyed that you're here! Did you know I've been praying for you? It's true. As this book has come together, I've prayed for the readers (that's YOU!) who will pick it up and begin this journey of the heart with me. So even as you're just starting out, you're already covered in prayer! That's a wonderful place to start. If I had it my way, we would all be meeting around a worktable in my art studio with our hands covered in paint, but this is almost as good.

As a young girl, you wouldn't find me on the playground playing in the sand or engaging in a rowdy game of kickball. You were more likely to find me wedged on a swing or sitting out in the grass with a notebook in my lap. My mom likes to say she couldn't keep me in composition notebooks because I would fill them so fast. Stories, poems, thoughts, and drawings were better than kickball. Then teenager Elaine started a "real journal" on the first day of her freshman year of high school and found that to be soothing to the soul. Replace fiction stories with nonfiction high school life and confessions of a young, misunderstood creative, and you've got yourself an idea of what I was scribbling down each day. Peppered throughout the tomes of my life were aspirational bits from magazines, collages, and drawings to illustrate what my heart couldn't communicate any other way.

These journals continued every day of high school through the first few days of college when life smacked me in the face and schoolwork became more demanding. But I still created art almost every day. Do you know why? I made time for it every day because I came to an understanding with the deep parts of my soul: Art is what I do. It's as simple as that. It was as necessary to me as getting dressed in the morning or brushing my teeth, and it served many purposes. It was a way to flush out those feelings I couldn't put into words; it was a tonic to heal what was broken; it was a happy place to remind me of who I was when I wasn't really sure. And it was a great partner to prayer.

The Lord makes all different kinds of people. Just like there are visual learners, there are people who need visual and tactile ways to feel. God is right there with you in the paint and paste and papers just as much as He's with you in the pew. So when we face challenges and strife, there's no shame in processing it right where you are. Some choose music, some choose writing, some choose art. And I will choose art again and again for as long as I'm able to hold a brush.

I hope you'll surrender yourself to our Father and allow yourself to really use the creative process as we encounter each topic in this book. For each week of the study, we'll look at the roadblocks and struggles we face as Christian women. Learning to surrender wholly as we face our struggles is what I want you to take away from these lessons. It might not happen overnight, but using the creative fire inside you is a perfect way to start the work.

Opening Prayer

Father God, as we prepare our hearts and minds to begin this study, I pray that You help us to surrender. Help us to give ourselves wholly and completely to the colorful path You have prepared for us. We are so undeserving of Your grace as we learn to face trouble with Your guidance instead of trying to tackle it alone. But You are good and have given us a creative spirit that we pray can be used to glorify You. Allow us to live according to Your will and experience Your peace that surpasses all understanding as we embark on this study together. In Your name we pray! Amen!

Day 1

Natural Light

When I was in college, clad in vintage skirts and hand screen-printed T-shirts, I was on the search for any course I could take that would spin my creative wheels while also giving me credit toward my degree. I stumbled upon Film Photography 101. It piqued my interest and gave me a brand new everyday accessory: a camera around my neck. I had stars in my eyes for developing my own wrinkly black and white prints and quickly learned the importance of natural light. It gave my photos life. My best pieces by far were exposures of my friends and family soaked in natural light, being their authentic selves. There are ways to fake good lighting by using studio lights or sometimes overexposing in the dark room, but there's really no true substitute for sunshine. It drives out the dark better than any artificial light source.

Parts of college were also dark, cloudy times for me. While I loved experimenting with new mediums and growing into the artist I am now, I had some scary lows centering around chronic worry and anxiety. My mind would do what I called at the time "cycling." It would revolve in cycles through stages of worry, despair, and half-hearted calm. I didn't know at the time that I was on the verge of being diagnosed with obsessive-compulsive disorder. The only thing I could do to fully drive out the bully in my brain was pray. I found that just like in my photography, I needed pure light to drive out darkness.

Take stock of your worries and anxieties today. Laying these things at the cross is the first step to relief from our worry!

The Lord Himself didn't waste any time in creating light for us. In fact, it was the second thing He did after first creating the heavens and the earth (Genesis 1:1–5). He turns darkness itself into light before the eyes of His believers (Isaiah 42:16). And above all, God gave the greatest, brightest light with the birth of Christ Jesus:

THE PEOPLE WHO WALKED IN DARKNESS HAVE SEEN A GREAT LIGHT; THOSE WHO DWELT IN A LAND OF DEEP DARKNESS, ON THEM HAS LIGHT SHONE.

ISAIAH 9:2 (ESV)

One of my favorite bits of the Book of Exodus is Moses leading the Israelites out of Egypt by way of the wilderness—often literally in the dark! What did God do? He did not abandon His people; He went before them and made Himself a pillar of fire to chase out the darkness and lead the way to the Promised Land (Exodus 13:20–22). That just strikes me as incredible.

What does this mean for us? It means that prayer is the only logical way to alleviate any type of darkness that surrounds you! When our hearts are worried, we can trust that the Lord will go before us, leading the way through our wilderness. He will provide brilliant natural light to illuminate our tangles and make the way easier to endure. This light can come in the form of peace, clarity, strength, or even just the knowledge of His presence.

How is God going before you and preparing the way for you through this wilderness? Write down some ways you see His hand at work.

Drawing near to Him drives out the lies of the enemy, just as light eradicates shadow, making our photos bright and clear—from our mess to His masterpiece.

1. Photograph yourself in your current state and include it in your Bible. Journal a prayer alongside it, asking the Lord to bring His light to drive out the worries that plague your heart.

2. Play with the idea of light and dark—find a way to represent it in your Bible. This could mean using the images of a sun and moon, or even could be as simple as a light color of paint vs. a dark color.

DAY 2

Bible Bookworm

Just call me Bookworm! It's true—I love reading. I treasure the feeling of getting wrapped up in a story, entangled in the plot, and being so perfectly invested in the characters. I've been known to read a novel in one day or even one sitting! But I have never read the Bible cover to cover. Have you? It's on my Bucket List for sure because I want to pay that sort of devotion to the most important book of all the books I've devoured in my life. But even though I haven't read it in its entirety, I can tell you with confidence something you WON'T find in the Bible: God telling you to worry or stress over something. I'll bet not once will you find the words: "Go ahead and worry so much you make yourself sick." Nope. In fact, *multiple times* in the Bible you'll find just the opposite advice: *Do not be anxious* (Philippians 4:6, NIV®).

But the truth is, we're human. And when we're in situations of high stress, we're the most human that humans can be because we lean into our emotions, which can make us worry and stress and doubt. We can read the Bible all we want, but our human emotions are hard to circumvent sometimes. Even the most devout and focused Christians find themselves in the throes of worry. So if any of this rings true to you, you're in good company.

So why is it so hard for us to follow the solid command *"do not be anxious"* in the Bible, when it's so easy to get sucked into a novel? We become enthralled with fantasies or mysteries, taking a deep interest in the next plot twist. We can recite our favorite passages from memory and have dreams of interacting with the dazzling characters! But *why* do we subconsciously fight the Word of God with worry and free-flowing tears of stress? After all, the Good Book contains stories that are *true* instead of head-in-the-clouds fiction! This is the way and the truth and the life we're talking about!

Let's consider Martha's story found in the Book of Luke. Poor little Martha! She invited Jesus into her home and wanted to make it a special occasion. She hustled and bustled in the kitchen, prepared a delicious meal, and served the Lord with intensity. While she was fluttering around stressed beyond reason (Hello! Jesus Himself was in her home!), her sister Mary sat at Jesus' feet listening to Him speak and teach. She was appalled that her sister was slacking off and not helping her serve her guest (Luke 10:38–40)! How rude! But the truth is, worry and anxiety were overshadowing her need for listening to Christ's teachings. Jesus said to her:

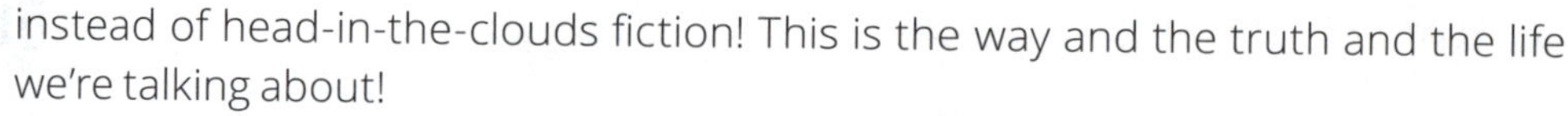

> "MARTHA, MARTHA, YOU ARE ANXIOUS AND TROUBLED ABOUT MANY THINGS, BUT ONE THING IS NECESSARY. MARY HAS CHOSEN THE GOOD PORTION, WHICH WILL NOT BE TAKEN AWAY FROM HER."
>
> LUKE 10:41–42 (ESV)

Are you Mary or Martha? Put yourself in their home in the presence of Christ Jesus and ask yourself if you're listening or serving.

____

____

____

____

I identify with Martha. I wish I could say I was like Mary, sitting at His feet, gazing starry-eyed at my Savior as He spoke, but I know I would be the sister stressing and worrying about being hospitable. In my mixed-up perspective, worry often equals showing my dedication and love. But WHY!? My need to hear the Lord's words ends up being overshadowed by the looming presence of this crippling anxiety! These human emotions become so overwhelming that I lean into them, no matter if they're rooted in truth or not. Mary is the wise sister, following the advice Jesus gave her.

____

____

____

____

Straight from the Lord Himself is the living Word. We should be digging into God's Word with enthusiasm just as we would the latest bestseller, the most exciting page-turner we've ever read! Listen as if Christ were sitting in our homes, teaching before our very eyes.

And he said to his disciples, "Therefore I tell you, do not be anxious about your life, what you will eat, nor about your body, what you will put on. For life is more than food, and the body more than clothing" (Luke 12:22–23, ESV).

____

____

____

Creative Heart Check:

1. Create a tip-in using a card and washi tape to make a little flap that opens like a book. Give your current feelings a book title and cover, then inside confess your worries to the Lord. Afterward, close the book on them and allow Him to carry them.

2. Make a creative bookmark for yourself with a favorite passage of Scripture. Use soothing colors that remind you to cast your cares on the Lord. Then place the bookmark in your Bible where you'll see it every day.

Day 3

Fixer-Upper

Before we found our current home, my husband and I house-hunted for months! I lost count of how many homes we toured. We looked at fixer-uppers, old historical homes, cute suburban places, and bonafide rural homesteads. Our search was very robust. We even found several we wanted to pursue! But the truth was that we knew nothing about construction, inspecting homes, or what to look for past the cosmetic look of a home. It was anxiety-inducing. We were worried we would unknowingly purchase a money pit or overlook something crucial. Lucky for us, we had a secret weapon: my dad. He has so much experience with contractor jobs, construction, and working with the bones of a house. He knows what to look for, what can be fixed, and what would be a fatal flaw in the foundation. If a cursory inspection didn't get past Dad, the house deal was dead in the water. I don't know what we would have done without him! I'm so fortunate to have so much wise counsel like that in my life. When I feel lost or like I'm in over my head, I have loved ones I can call on who have been through similar situations.

The truth is, there's a sort of stigma around asking for help or advice. For some reason it can be perceived as a weakness, which simply isn't true. Recognizing when our weary hearts need help and asking for someone to come alongside us is a sign of strength.

Read Proverbs 24:6. What does the Bible say about seeking advice?

We need others who have more experience than we do to come in and advise us in what to do next. We often don't get any say in the matter when the anxious thoughts creep in; they manifest very quickly. When they come, the thoughts set up camp and start to unpack. I used to believe that if I wasn't overthinking and worrying about something, I was telling God it didn't matter to me. Like I wasn't doing my part. So I would let the worry go uninterrupted and bear the burden. But the reality is that worry isn't a good house guest or neighbor. It has nothing nice to say and doesn't add any positivity or virtue to our existence. When the overthinking starts to build, it's essential to bring in an expert to evaluate the situation and tell us what works, what doesn't, and which parts are detrimental.

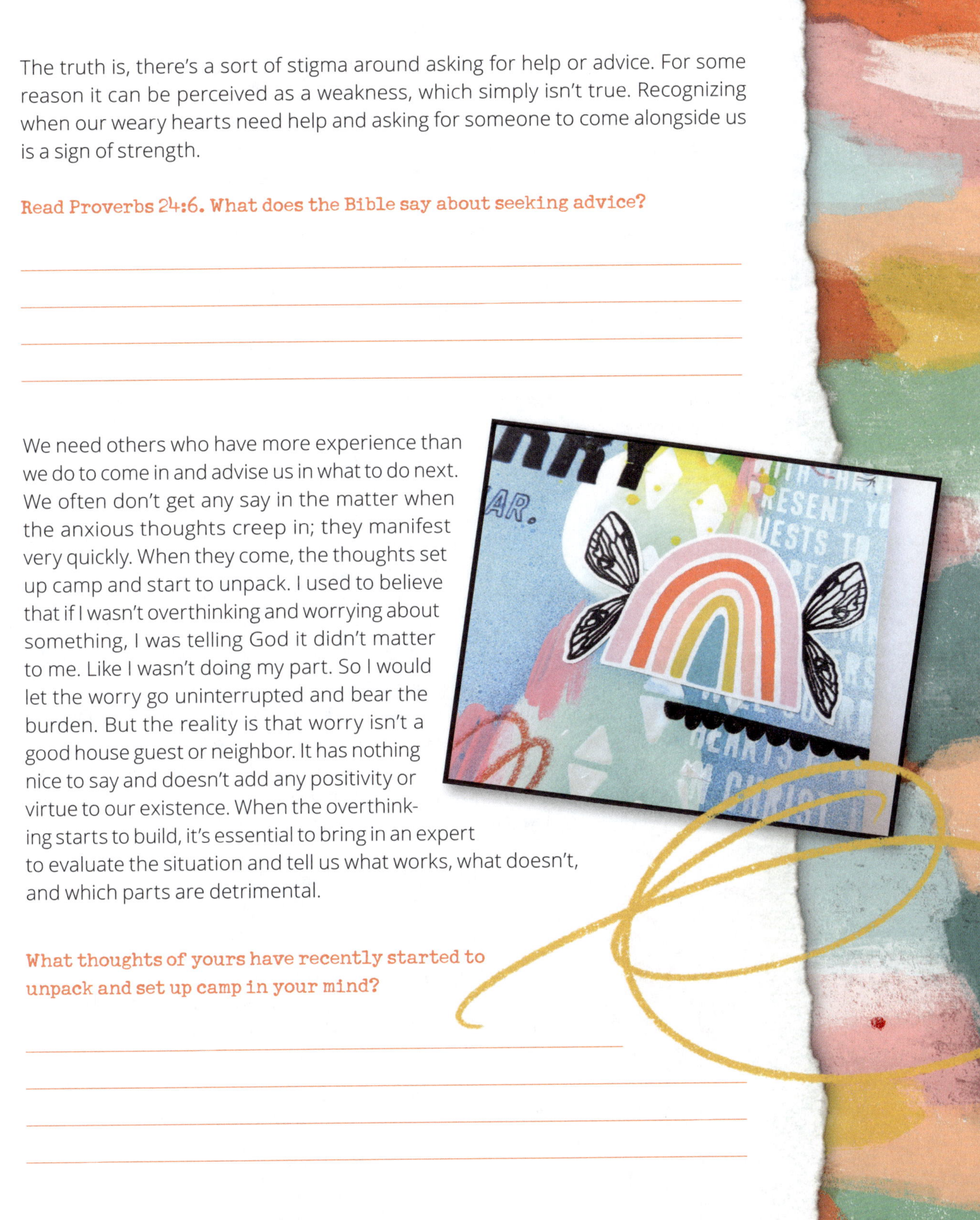

What thoughts of yours have recently started to unpack and set up camp in your mind?

There's something to be said for community because, as humans, we're not meant to shoulder our burden alone, especially when our hearts are heavy with worry. I'm sure you've heard the quote, "It takes a village to raise a child." Well, the same is true for children of God. You might think that wise counsel has to be a parent, but that's not the case. It can be anyone who has experience and true wisdom in what you're going through and can advise you moving forward. The Lord fills our lives with people to lean on when we're overwhelmed, confused, or anxious. Your wise counsel might be an elder in your church, a doctor, a family member, a best friend, or a therapist. As long as they have your very best interest at heart and are trustworthy, prayerfully allow them to weigh in.

What can we learn about the importance of community from Ecclesiastes 4:12? Make a list of people in your life you can seek out for wise counsel when you need it.

Now that we've been living in our house for over three years, one of my favorite things is to look out our bedroom window at the willow tree in the backyard. The sunshine peeks through the branches, and I can't help but have so much gratitude for the village that helped shape our home. Our fixer-upper and the hearts inside it are the product of so much love, prayer, and wise counsel.

Creative Heart Check:

1. Echo the number 3 in your entry (ex: use 3 of the same elements or feature a large number 3, etc.) to symbolize a cord of 3 strands from Ecclesiastes 4:12 and journal about the community God has provided you.

2. Create a Bible entry with a bold title of the last good advice you were given.

DAY 4
Little and Loved

This is a little story about true childlike faith. As a child, my family went to church every Sunday. We attended a small church, the kind where everybody knew everybody, you know? Each Sunday our minister included a segment in our service for joys and concerns. Anyone in the congregation could pipe up with a praise point or something for everyone to add to their prayer list. These were mostly big things, like the overwhelming joy of a new baby in the family or a request for prayer for a military deployment. But one Sunday from a pew near the front came a tiny voice. It was my 5-year-old sister Anna saying that her goldfish died, and she needed prayers. The congregation laughed, my mother was equal parts amused and mortified, but our minister was gravely concerned. I think most people would have just chalked it up as an adorable interruption to the serious requests, but he didn't do that. He added Anna to the prayer list and said that there was no prayer too small for God. I can't say for sure, but I think her little 5-year-old self felt important and heard that day.

What joys and concerns do you have for the Lord today?

____

____

____

____

I often edit my prayer list in my head (which is silly because God knows everything we're thinking before we think it!) before I "officially" bring it to the Lord. I think about all the struggle and strife in the world and often decide that a worry of mine is comparatively inconsequential. How can God Almighty care about my small medical issue when people's loved ones are dying somewhere in the world? How can my little work problem compare to the political turmoil being experienced in many countries? My worries are in an entirely different ballpark than the major league problems worldwide. But friend, if it's important to you—if it feels like a heavy worry in your world—it's important to God. In Scripture, 1 Peter 5:7 tells us to cast all our anxieties on Him. The Bible doesn't instruct us to only give the big worries to Him; it says ALL—even the small ones.

Read Matthew 6:25–27. What instruction are we given in the first sentence? In order to abide by this, we must give our worries to the Lord no matter how small they are!

____

____

____

____

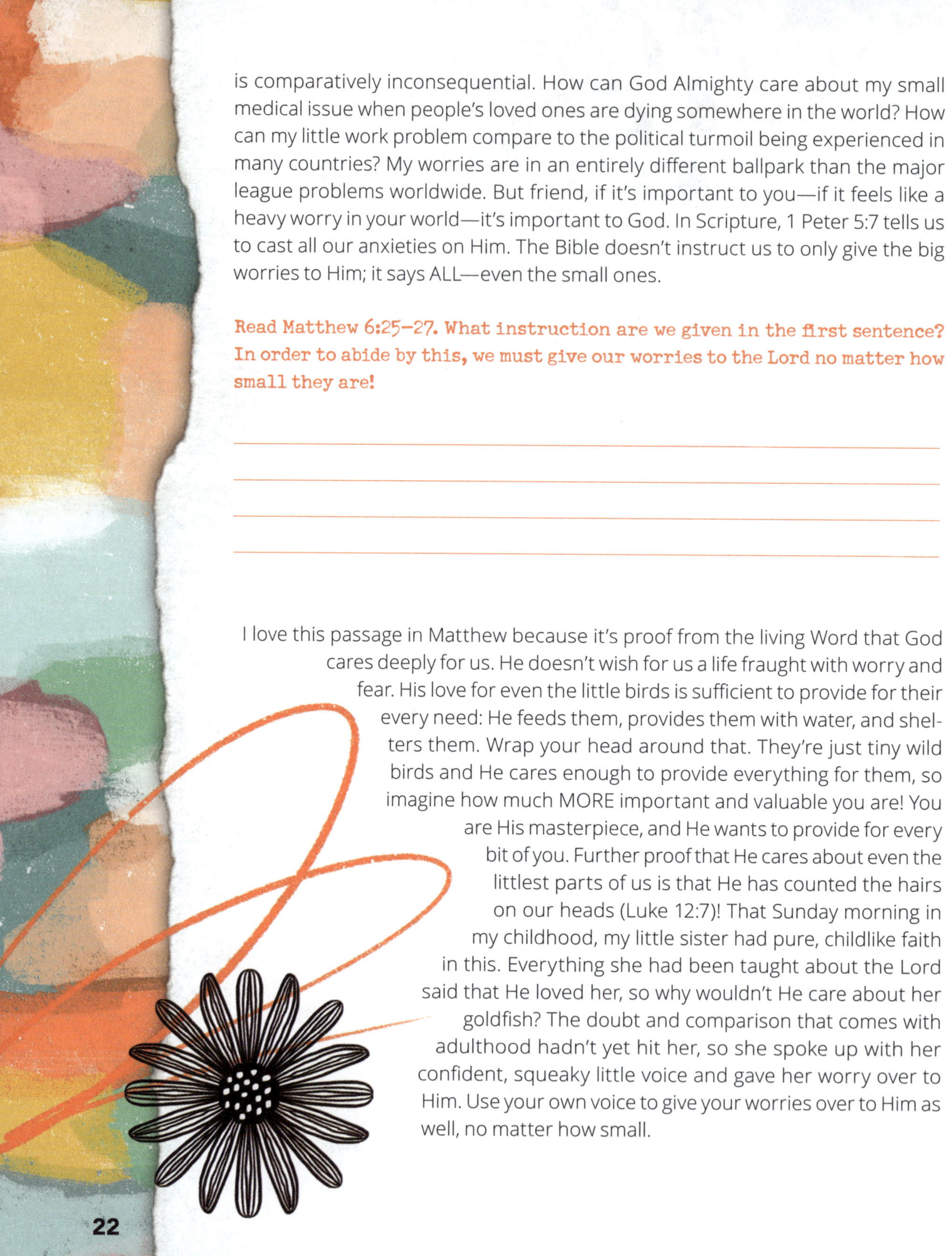

I love this passage in Matthew because it's proof from the living Word that God cares deeply for us. He doesn't wish for us a life fraught with worry and fear. His love for even the little birds is sufficient to provide for their every need: He feeds them, provides them with water, and shelters them. Wrap your head around that. They're just tiny wild birds and He cares enough to provide everything for them, so imagine how much MORE important and valuable you are! You are His masterpiece, and He wants to provide for every bit of you. Further proof that He cares about even the littlest parts of us is that He has counted the hairs on our heads (Luke 12:7)! That Sunday morning in my childhood, my little sister had pure, childlike faith in this. Everything she had been taught about the Lord said that He loved her, so why wouldn't He care about her goldfish? The doubt and comparison that comes with adulthood hadn't yet hit her, so she spoke up with her confident, squeaky little voice and gave her worry over to Him. Use your own voice to give your worries over to Him as well, no matter how small.

Do you have worries that seem too small for God? Write them down and lay them at the cross!

____

____

____

____

Creative Heart Check:

1. Use a little bird, a goldfish, or another small creature to symbolize God caring for your worries, even the smallest ones.

2. Recall a time in your childhood (or adulthood!) that the Lord took care of your small worries. Tell that story in your Bible and use it to inspire childlike illustrations (scribbles, crayon marks, stick figures, etc.).

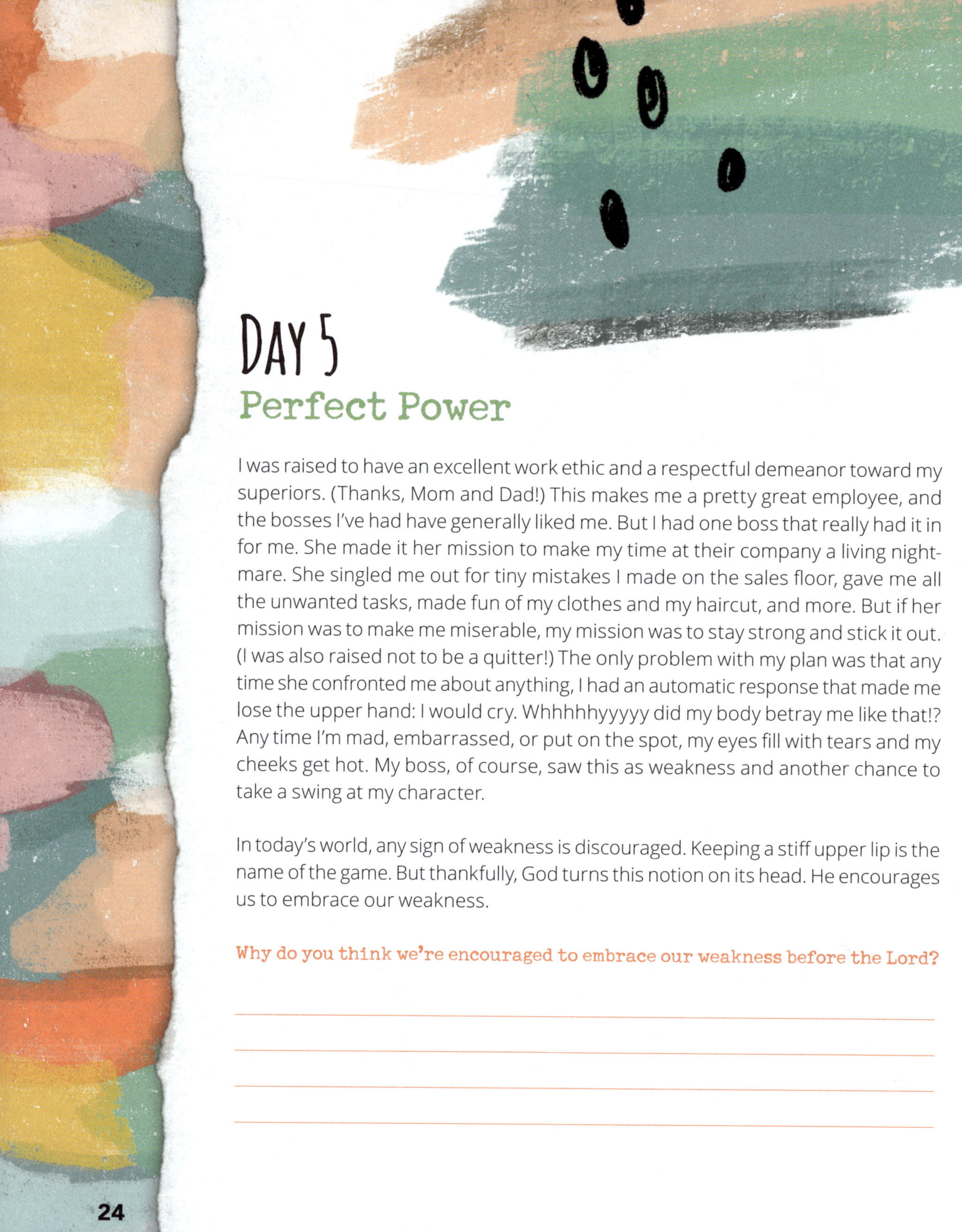

Day 5
Perfect Power

I was raised to have an excellent work ethic and a respectful demeanor toward my superiors. (Thanks, Mom and Dad!) This makes me a pretty great employee, and the bosses I've had have generally liked me. But I had one boss that really had it in for me. She made it her mission to make my time at their company a living nightmare. She singled me out for tiny mistakes I made on the sales floor, gave me all the unwanted tasks, made fun of my clothes and my haircut, and more. But if her mission was to make me miserable, my mission was to stay strong and stick it out. (I was also raised not to be a quitter!) The only problem with my plan was that any time she confronted me about anything, I had an automatic response that made me lose the upper hand: I would cry. Whhhhhyyyyy did my body betray me like that!? Any time I'm mad, embarrassed, or put on the spot, my eyes fill with tears and my cheeks get hot. My boss, of course, saw this as weakness and another chance to take a swing at my character.

In today's world, any sign of weakness is discouraged. Keeping a stiff upper lip is the name of the game. But thankfully, God turns this notion on its head. He encourages us to embrace our weakness.

Why do you think we're encouraged to embrace our weakness before the Lord?

If you're having trouble coming up with an answer, I'll tell you the reason: God Himself fights for us (Exodus 14:14) and is strong when we are weak. Even though we are repeatedly commanded to be strong throughout the Bible, the Lord knows we are human beings and we are inherently weak. We gain strength through Him alone! Second Corinthians 12:9 (ESV) says:

My grace is sufficient for you, for my power is made perfect in weakness.

Read that again—His power is made PERFECT in our WEAKNESS! Praise God, because we've got that in spades!

Read the entirety of 2 Corinthians 12:8–10. What parts stand out to you?

According to Scripture, we should embrace our weakness and even boast about it (2 Corinthians 12:9, ESV) so that we can be wrapped fully in God's power and strength! Looking at the last verse of this passage, it says plainly to be "content with weaknesses, insults, hardships, persecutions, and calamities" (2 Corinthians 12:10, ESV). Reflecting on that horrible boss I had, I think those things directly applied to my situation.

____

____

____

____

As Christians, we're called to fully rely on Him. I love thinking back to times when I was weak and picturing a hedge of protection and strength around me. How funny that when we feel we're at our lowest and most vulnerable, we're actually the strongest because His power within us is made perfect. We allow that strength to fill us when we embrace the weak. All I have to say about that is that God is so good.

Write down your weaknesses and prayerfully ask the Lord to help you accept and embrace them in His name.

____

____

____

____

Creative Heart Check:

1. Create a circle. Fill half of the circle with your weaknesses and fill the other half with ways the Lord fills you with His perfect power. This will symbolize how we are made whole through Him.

2. Journal the lyrics to the song, "Jesus Loves Me."

Day 1
Name It and Claim It

When I was in the thick of my senior year of college, I was diagnosed with obsessive-compulsive disorder (OCD). The diagnosis was completely out of the blue...but then again it really shouldn't have been a shock. I had always been a force of worry and fear and playing things on the safe side. There was an order to the way I liked things and a definite sequence to my life. While I was an extremely creative girl, the "rules" were always black and white to me. My parents never gave it a second thought—"That's just Elaine being Elaine!" I was...quirky. But once I hit college, my mental health started to affect my everyday life. My fears would take over my day and come out in unhealthy behaviors that would make me miss classes or put a strain on my relationships. Hello, OCD. After my diagnosis I started seeing a therapist who gave me an assignment to keep a notebook each day of things that affected my day or put me into a panic. It forced me to confront the roots of my compulsions and recognize patterns in my fears and anxieties. I also learned something valuable: the difference between anxiety and fear.

What affected your day today, either positively or negatively? Can you recognize any patterns from yesterday and today that tell a story about your state of being?

____

____

____

____

Knowing the difference between these two is a tricky thing because they so often go hand in hand. Fear is an emotion caused by the belief that an interaction, experience, or threat will be dangerous or painful. I believe that anxiety is sort

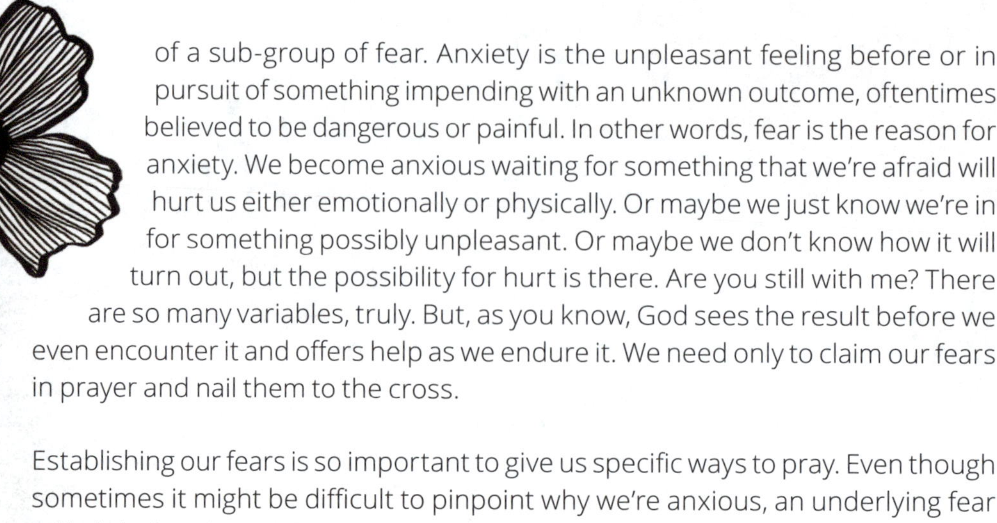

of a sub-group of fear. Anxiety is the unpleasant feeling before or in pursuit of something impending with an unknown outcome, oftentimes believed to be dangerous or painful. In other words, fear is the reason for anxiety. We become anxious waiting for something that we're afraid will hurt us either emotionally or physically. Or maybe we just know we're in for something possibly unpleasant. Or maybe we don't know how it will turn out, but the possibility for hurt is there. Are you still with me? There are so many variables, truly. But, as you know, God sees the result before we even encounter it and offers help as we endure it. We need only to claim our fears in prayer and nail them to the cross.

Establishing our fears is so important to give us specific ways to pray. Even though sometimes it might be difficult to pinpoint why we're anxious, an underlying fear is likely lurking beneath the surface. After time in therapy, I discovered that many of my own personal anxieties are fueled by a fear of dying or my loved ones dying. That was a hard realization to admit out loud as a Christian, because I know dying means going to my heavenly home and being closer to the Lord. Nevertheless, I'm working through a fear there every day. Acknowledging that fear allows me to claim it before the Lord and pray about it specifically!

What fears do you have that you can name, claim, and nail to the cross?

God will never shame you or forsake you in the wake of your fears. Quite the opposite actually. Isaiah 41:8–10 tells us that God is always with us through whatever makes us afraid.

> FEAR NOT, FOR I AM WITH YOU; BE NOT DISMAYED,
> FOR I AM YOUR GOD; I WILL STRENGTHEN YOU, I WILL HELP YOU,
> I WILL UPHOLD YOU WITH MY RIGHTEOUS RIGHT HAND.
>
> ISAIAH 41:10 (ESV)

Naming our fears makes us all the more ready to receive strength from the Lord. It helps us look to Him in our time of weakness, knowing from where our help comes (Psalm 121). Even if the thing we fear is a painful outcome, our Father will be there even then.

Creative Heart Check:

1. Write down your greatest fears on a piece of paper, then seal them in an envelope and attach in your Bible. This is you claiming your fears and giving them over to God!

2. Create a collage of your fears. Use paint, images, stencils, and text to represent what fears you want to overcome.

DAY 2
Fight or Flight

Raise your hand if you've ever wanted to just run away from your fears instead of facing them. I think just about everyone who's reading this book will have raised their hand at that. Maybe it means avoiding certain people or situations. Or maybe it means literally hiding under the covers and not coming out to face the day. That's often the easiest thing to do, right? It's fight or flight. Unfortunately, running, hiding, and slamming the door isn't the answer to our problems—on the other side of that locked door, our fear is still waiting for us. I've been there myself on numerous occasions. There were early times in our marriage where my husband and I faced financial setback after setback; we were living paycheck to paycheck in a shoddy apartment barely scraping by. We were scared. Bills just kept rolling in, and I wanted nothing more than to hide under the covers and ignore them. But I knew running from what we were facing would only make things worse. So we worked hard and we prayed...a lot. We prayed for strength, contentment, peace, and financial opportunities.

Flipping through the Bible, you can find cautionary tales of people who tried to run from their problems, from their fears, or from God's calling on their life. I mean, Jonah tried to run from God, and we all know what happened to him! (Jonah 1)

One story that stands out to me is that of Hagar. She was the servant of Sarai, later renamed Sarah, and the concubine of Abram, later renamed Abraham. When Sarai couldn't conceive, she ordered Hagar to lay with Abram and they quickly conceived a son. Sarai was bitter and resented Hagar, so she started treating her poorly. The Bible says she "dealt harshly" with Hagar even in her pregnancy! It's not clear what that means exactly, but one could assume mistreatment, verbal abuse, or even physical abuse. So Hagar ran. She had to get out of there. Away from the poor treatment, away from her problems, away from the fear.

What emotions and feelings do you think motivated Hagar to run?

But after her escape, an angel of the Lord met Hagar at a spring of water in the wilderness, and she got a harsh reality check. He told her to return to face her mistress, deliver her baby to Abram and Sarai, and her offspring would be multiplied. Um, wow. Who wants to hear orders to go back to the place they narrowly escaped? That was probably the last thing she wanted to hear. But despite her direct orders to go back the way she came, Hagar felt comforted by the Lord's presence.

It's amazing the comfort, encouragement, and resolve one can feel with the knowledge that the Lord is near. We begin to feel like we have what it takes to face what's to come. God hasn't called us to live in fear; He's called us to face our fears with strength and courage through Christ!

Creative Heart Check:

1. Illustrate or collage a figure of a woman to represent Hagar and her journey with fear. Journal the ways you relate to her story.

2. Use images of feet, socks, or shoes to symbolize standing your ground in strength to face your fears with the Lord's help.

Day 3
Heart Work

Imagine me three months pregnant, hearing the doctor tell us that there might be something wrong with the baby. We had a whole host of tests run—blood draws, finger pricks, scans, genetic testing—I was feeling like a walking science experiment. Several of the tests came back inconclusive, which led our doctor to believe that there was a genetic abnormality. A little background information about our pregnancy—we struggled with infertility. We tried and tried for over seven YEARS to conceive a baby to no avail, until we finally sought fertility treatments to facilitate a conception. Our attachment to this little jellybean was ironclad, but with that upsetting news, we felt our hope slipping away from us. I was terrified. I felt like every move I made would make him worse; he just seemed so fragile. There was nothing to do but repeat the tests and wait.

I lay in bed and sleep wouldn't come. I just thought about our precious little guy and the experiences he might never have. I prayed and prayed until I was so tired the words didn't make sense. Then suddenly an overwhelming sense of peace came over me. I felt content and confident that everything would work out. I no longer feared for the baby in that moment but felt hopeful and full of gratitude. God delivered me from my fear that night in such a big and obvious way; it was surreal. I'll always remember that night and include it as a powerful part of my testimony.

Looking back on that moment, I can't help but marvel at God's willingness to comfort us at all times. There's no inconvenient time to cry out to Him in worry or fear. Psalm 34:4 (ESV) says, *I sought the LORD, and he answered me and delivered me from all my fears.* No matter where you are, what you're doing, or what time of day it is, He's available to calm your restless heart. There's no need to save your prayers for the end of the day or a special time you set aside. You can reach for the Lord any time you need His comfort and joy.

I think it's also worth noting that the Lord is doing much more than calming us in these powerful moments: He's actively fighting for you. Part of the reason our hearts can rest is because God is working in the wait and His work is never done. He is sovereign and has His hand in every detail of your life. In my story, God was calming my heart, but He was also helping my husband to be a supportive partner, guiding the lab technicians to clarity, keeping my unborn child safe and warm, giving our doctor the right words to deliver the results, and on and on. There's so much the Lord is providing that we can't fathom the intricacies of

His power. It's not our right nor our burden to understand everything He does, but He fights for us nonetheless.

Look at Exodus 14:13–16. In this passage, Moses is relaying words from God to the Israelites. He tells them,

"DO NOT BE AFRAID. STAND FIRM AND YOU WILL SEE THE DELIVERANCE THE LORD WILL BRING YOU TODAY."

EXODUS 14:13 (NIV®)

He tells them to stand strong in faith, and the Lord will calm their fears! Now look specifically at Exodus 14:14. It's a short verse, but one with so much truth and power.

Write out this passage and underline or highlight the bits that stand out to you.

____

____

____

____

Exodus 14:14 is my "life verse." It's the passage of Scripture by which I live my life, one that I recall repeatedly in times of need. These are the very words that bring me comfort when I feel myself spinning out of control.

Do you have a life verse? Do you have a verse that brings you comfort even in the worst of times? Proclaim it here!

____

____

____

____

Even as I write this paragraph, I thank our Father for His perfect power in calming the storm when it seems hopeless. I thank Him for my son who was born a perfect 7 lbs 8 oz bundle of pure sunshine. I thank Him for always being near to us and standing with us. When our fears seem too big, He is bigger.

Creative Heart Check:

1. Flip through the Bible to your life verse and use it for a creative entry!

2. Use the title, "This is My Story," for a Bible entry. Choose an important part of your testimony to journal about on this page.

DAY 4
First Aid

Little ones can be fearless. If you're a parent or an older sibling, you might be able to vouch for me on this. I have a 2-year-old son, and I'm always amazed at what he gets into. He climbs and jumps on things with unsteady balance and gives me gray hair. He sleeps in his crib in the pitch black, no problem. He might catch a glimpse of something scary on TV and doesn't bat an eye. It baffles me.

Recently my husband and I woke up in the morning to frantic crying from our son's nursery. We ran in to see him lying on the floor with a bloody nose, screaming for dear life. He must have tried to climb out of his crib, lost his balance, and fallen face-first onto the floor. He obviously hit hard because blood was just pouring out of his nose. Poor little guy. He reached for me, wanting comfort, waiting for the "ouch" to pass. We got him cleaned up, gave him a cuddle, and fifteen minutes later he was back to his ornery self.

You'd think that after taking a tumble, my son would have learned something about doing stunts like this, but that same day he was climbing and jumping on the couch like nothing had happened. He's so little! Where does this confidence and courage come from!?

After you suffer a setback or a hard season, are you likely to get back up on the horse? Or are you overly cautious for a while? Are you more likely to lean into the Lord, or do you shy away?

I think the reason my son is so bold after a "crash and burn" is because he trusts me and trusts his father to care for him. He trusts us 100 percent to protect him from major harm. (No pressure or anything, right?) Even though we might not be able to stop every single hurt from happening, we're always a few steps away to swoop in and comfort him. As humans, we have certain instincts, but much of how we react to situations are learned responses, including fear. What my son has learned in his short two years of life is that Mama and Daddy always show up.

It's not hard to see where I'm going with this, is it? Our Heavenly Father always shows up. If we suffer hurt, He's there to comfort us. If we fall, He comes to remind us that nothing is too far gone to save—He still has a use for us. We're not judged for our fears, but rather by our faith in our Father amidst those fears.

Psalm 27:1–2 (NIV®) says,

The Lord is my light and my salvation—whom shall I fear? The Lord is the stronghold of my life—of whom shall I be afraid?

When the wicked advance against me to devour me, it is my enemies and my foes who will stumble and fall. Right there in black and white are the words, "whom shall I fear?" As long as we have faith in our Lord and Savior, then who should we fear at all? Nothing and no one is bigger or more powerful than our God! Our fear implies that we aren't confident in the Lord's abilities and might! Who are we to question His divine power and plan (Isaiah 55:8–9)?

Contemplate 2 Samuel 22:2–3. It describes God as a solid rock and a strong fortress. What other comparisons can you form about the Lord?

If there's one thing I want you to take away from this, it's that fear is a waste of time and anguish. The Lord is already working on whatever troubles you. Knowing that He has power over all can be your deliverance. Don't let the fear of hurt stop you from living out His calling on your life! He will be there to scoop you up and comfort you no matter how far you fall.

Creative Heart Check:

1. Illustrate a broken jar that's been put back together. "Fill" the cracks with paint to symbolize how God still uses us even when we've been broken.

2. Journal out some of your past hurts and make note of how the Lord delivered you from your fears.

Day 5
Suit Up

I'm a very organized person. (Okay, that's an understatement.) But if you looked in my purse…it's kind of a mess. On the bright side, it has everything you would ever need in there! Coupons, hand sanitizer, wet wipes, my inhaler, three lip balms, two pens, my wallet, a tiny little flashlight—the list goes on and on. Not to mention it contains my phone, which is practically my lifeline. It's my connection to work, family, 911, my grocery list, my camera, my reminder alarms…. I would be lost without it. I've left the house without my phone before, and I felt vulnerable. What if I had an emergency? How would I call for help? What if a member of my family had an emergency and they tried to call me? It just felt like I was asking for trouble, being without it. My purse contains all the items to make my life easier and more comfortable when I'm on the go.

What things are always in your purse or car that you never leave home without? How would you feel if you accidentally left something important behind?

But the truth is, we get too reliant on these material possessions of ours. There was a time when cell phones didn't exist—in fact, I remember that point in time! No one had one and somehow we made it work, right? We didn't need an alarm on our phones to remind us to take our medicine; we just remembered. We didn't find it necessary to text a photo of our restaurant meal to our cousin. We certainly weren't scrolling social media while we were out with friends—we were actually being social!

My point is that much of what we rely on, especially electronics, aren't actually true necessities. Yet we cling to them as if they are protecting us in some way. We walk out the door each morning with all the essentials in tow. I mean, my husband carries a backpack to work most days! But there are things we should never leave home without, and you can't carry them in a purse. I'm talking about the armor of God.

This armor is not made of iron or steel; it's made of your faith in the Lord. It protects us from the enemy as we go about our days, and it reminds us that we are children of God.

Read Ephesians 6:10–18. Now list out the pieces of our suit of armor we should put on each day.

We've been talking for the last four days about fear, and the armor of God includes six tools we can use to actively combat it. We are warriors. We are in the Lord's army, and each day we march into battle to slay the lies of the enemy and spread the truth of the gospel! We can't do either of those things while carrying around a spirit of fear! How can we hold our sword of the Spirit and our shield of faith while carrying a cumbersome helping of our own insecurities and fear of what comes next? I know it might not happen overnight, but we need to take steps to put down these fears so that we can make room for the full armor of God.

____

____

____

____

____

I want to focus on one piece of the armor in particular: the shield of faith. Every piece of the armor is important, but this one is non-negotiable. The shield of faith is our first line of defense against fear. Our faith in the Lord Almighty is quite literally the foundation on which we should build our lives. Holding up that shield protects us when we are tempted to doubt God's power. Letting that shield drop leaves us vulnerable to the fiery arrows of evil and lies. We can't ever be caught unaware. The enemy waits for us to leave ourselves undefended and takes the opportunity to strike when we're at our weakest. Each day we have to confidently hold up the shield of faith knowing beyond a shadow of a doubt that the Lord is sovereign and Jesus is King. So for heaven's sake: Put down your phone and pick up that shield, friend!

Creative Heart Check:

1. Create a shield design for yourself. Include symbols and images of things God has given you to make you feel strong.

2. Draw arrows on your page and label them with lies from the enemy.

Week 3
comparison

Day 1
Click of Approval

I used to do #allthethings and do them with aplomb. I had a to-do list each morning and didn't go to bed until everything was crossed off. It felt good to lie down at night, knowing I completed my list to perfection and everything was in order. I held my co-workers, friends, and family members to this same standard. It was hard for me to rely on anyone else to get things done the right way and on time. Many days at work, people would miss deadlines, and it frustrated me to no end. I was certain that it was possible to get things done in a timely manner because I was doing it! All you had to do was make a list and manage your time. That wasn't so hard, right? I didn't used to think so. I would log on to social media and post beautiful photos of my home cleaned to perfection, my cute outfits, and many, many projects I would complete each week. It was a true depiction of the life I was living…. Then I had a child.

Having a baby brought me down to a more human level of productivity. I had to relinquish some responsibilities at work because I simply couldn't complete all the things I used to do. (Embarrassing!) I had to delegate. (Cringe!) I had to accept that I was human and no longer Superwoman. (Cue the tears.) On social media, it would look like I had everything together on the screen, but in reality there were days I didn't have time to even write out the to-do list! I would take a photo of a clean house, but really it was just one clean corner and stuff shoved out of frame so I could get the shot. My outfits turned into leggings, soft oversized shirts, and a topknot. The projects I used to do were nonexistent. But as far as anyone else knew, life was business as usual.

I would look at my peers on photo-sharing apps—friends with four or five kids—and wonder how they managed to hold it together. They would show photos of the cooking-show-worthy breakfast they made, gym bods, or gorgeous completed house projects. Their accounts really just made me feel bad about myself.

Have you ever found yourself feeling inadequate compared to your friends on social media? What sort of emotions does it evoke? (i.e.: jealousy, anger, etc.)

The reality is—their accounts, much like mine, only show the peaks of their week, not the falls. Most people don't post their biggest life flops for all the world to see. No one wants the internet to know about the big fight with their spouse, that their kid acted up in a restaurant, or that their guest bathroom has been under construction for over a year. They only post the good things. They are likely struggling to do life, just like you. Most people on social media are just posting their highlights for the approval of their peers.

Galatians 1:10 (ESV) might have a real wake-up call for you. While preaching the gospel, Apostle Paul refused to alter the doctrine of Christ to appease men. Here's the verse:

> FOR AM I NOW SEEKING THE APPROVAL OF MAN, OR OF GOD? OR AM I TRYING TO PLEASE MAN? IF I WERE STILL TRYING TO PLEASE MAN, I WOULD NOT BE A SERVANT OF CHRIST.

Write down your initial reaction to that Scripture passage!

We can't water down the Scriptures to please others, and we certainly shouldn't alter who we are for the acceptance of our peers! We shouldn't be seeking their approval. As disciples, we're only seeking the approval of Christ, and He already loves us for who we are! He doesn't compare us to one another, nor should we. We're each individuals with our own stories to tell.

In this digital age of social media, it's so easy to fall into the pit of wanting approval. It's easier than ever before because we have a window into the lives of others at our fingertips! Not to mention we're all imperfect beings; these photo feeds depicting perfect lives are false. We put way too much weight on the number of "likes" we get and forget about the love we receive from Christ Jesus. That's the real reward!

In what ways can you make your social media presence (if you have one) more authentic and use it to share the gospel instead? Can you make it less about comparison and more about acceptance?

Creative Heart Check:

1. Share a photo of your Bible entry and write a caption for it in the form of a prayer.

2. Illustrate an image of your favorite electronic device and ask God to help you incorporate peace and gratitude into your heart surrounding it instead of the temptation to compare your life to others'.

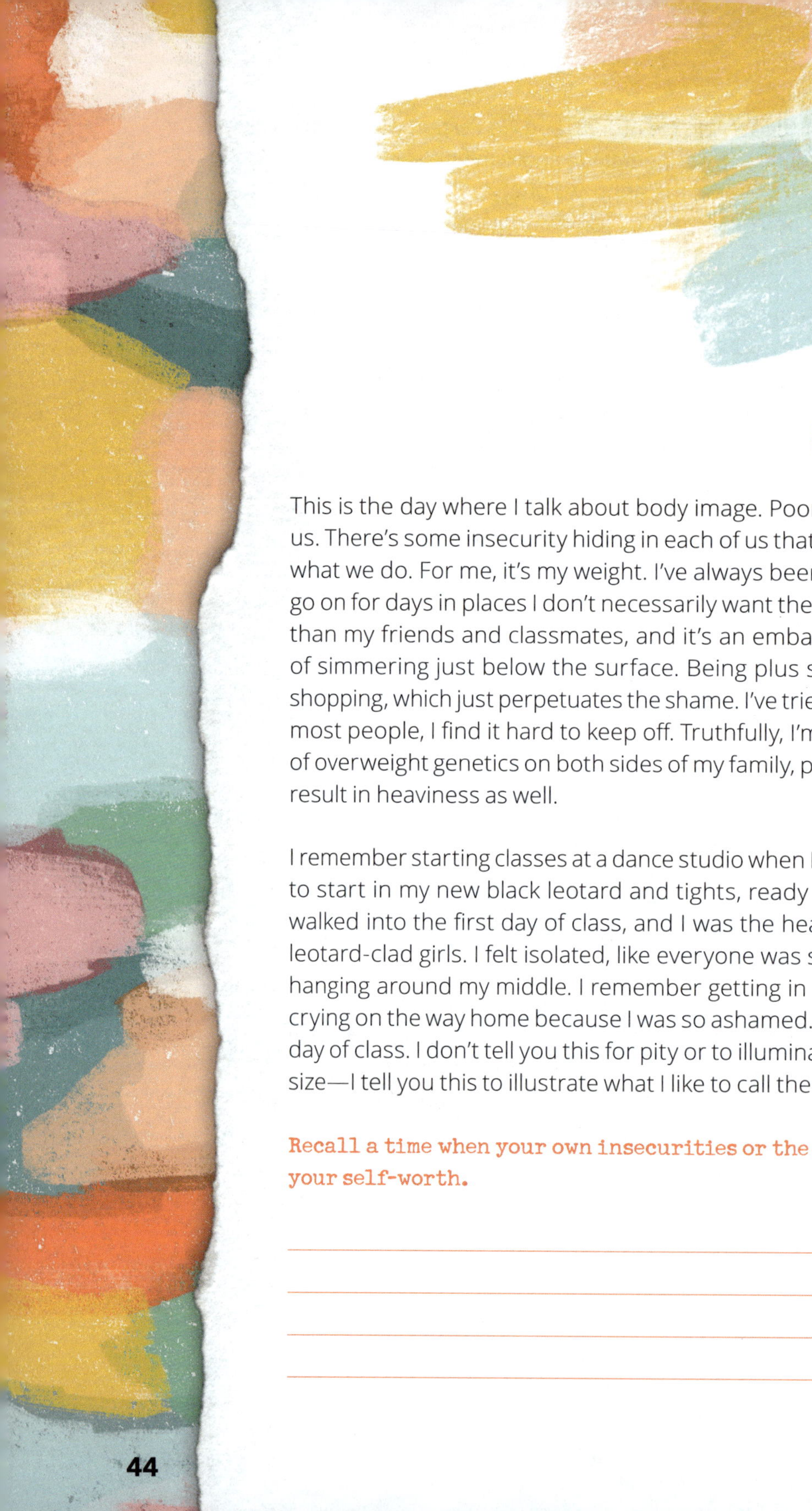

Day 2
Shame Spiral

This is the day where I talk about body image. Poor body image plagues most of us. There's some insecurity hiding in each of us that we just can't shake no matter what we do. For me, it's my weight. I've always been...let's call it curvy. My curves go on for days in places I don't necessarily want them. Ha! I've always been bigger than my friends and classmates, and it's an embarrassment that is always sort of simmering just below the surface. Being plus size makes it hard to even go shopping, which just perpetuates the shame. I've tried losing weight before, but like most people, I find it hard to keep off. Truthfully, I'm working against generations of overweight genetics on both sides of my family, plus multiple health issues that result in heaviness as well.

I remember starting classes at a dance studio when I was fourteen. I was so excited to start in my new black leotard and tights, ready to try something new. Then I walked into the first day of class, and I was the heaviest one there out of all the leotard-clad girls. I felt isolated, like everyone was staring at the extra poundage hanging around my middle. I remember getting in my mom's car after class and crying on the way home because I was so ashamed. I wanted to quit after just one day of class. I don't tell you this for pity or to illuminate the struggles of being plus size—I tell you this to illustrate what I like to call the shame spiral.

Recall a time when your own insecurities or the scrutiny of others affected your self-worth.

Who told me being overweight was an ugly thing? Who told me I had reason to be ashamed? Probably a classmate or an episode of a '90s sitcom, who knows. But the result is a never-ending spiral of shame and poor body image. And who on this earth has the authority to make someone feel that way about themselves?

Adam and Eve encountered a similar situation in the Garden of Eden! During the Fall in Genesis 3, after Eve ate the fruit, they heard the Lord walking in the garden, and they hid themselves because they suddenly felt ashamed of their nakedness. And the Lord God asked them a loaded question:

"WHO TOLD YOU THAT YOU WERE NAKED?"
GENESIS 3:11 (ESV)

What He really meant was: "Who made you feel ashamed of your bodies? My love and acceptance are the only approval you need."

Regarding the instance you outlined in the previous question: Who initiated the shame spiral for you? Ask yourself if your insecurity and shame was biblical or imposed by the world.

____

____

____

____

The short answer is that if it doesn't come from God's Word, it's not righteous. The Word tells us over and over that we're beautiful and made in God's own image.

(Genesis 1:27, Psalm 139:14, Ephesians 4:24) So when we are criticizing ourselves in an endless spiral of shame, we're also criticizing the Lord and His handiwork.

Furthermore, hiding any part of ourselves from the Lord is fruitless. (Get it? Adam and Eve ate the fruit?) He has seen our innermost parts and knit them together Himself. He sees all, so we have no need to hide who we are or what we look like from God.

What is the message of Hebrews 4:13?

____

____

____

If you're wondering how my dance career turned out, my mom and dad told me that my size had nothing to do with my abilities or my worth and told me to finish what I started. (Way to go, Mom and Dad!) As it turns out, they were right. I was asked to be a part of the studio's competitive team of dancers that performed at events and national competitions. It also led to four more years of dancing on another team at my high school as well as in our theater productions. Every time I danced, I climbed further and further out of that shame spiral because it was clear God had bigger plans for me than I had for myself. Twenty years later, I'm still climbing. I still have setbacks, but it takes me much less time to recover because I know from Scripture that I am worthy.

Creative Heart Check:

1. Illustrate the word "BEAUTIFUL" in huge letters across your entire Bible page or art journal page. It needs no journaling, the word speaks for itself—captioning your body, your personality, and your life.

2. Draw a messy spiral or tornado on your page and journal about your own shame spiral and how it's affected your life. Be sure to cap it off with biblical truths about who God says you are!

Share the Sunshine

Let's address a topic that we have ALL encountered at one point or another: jealousy. It's ugly. It's nasty. It's rude. And it sure isn't biblical. But our hearts are sometimes clogged with it anyway, and comparison is the root cause. When we start comparing our lives to others', it breeds jealousy. Let's lay out a scenario:

Your close friend calls you and says, "We're moving!" What exciting news! You're so happy that her family is going to have more space and will be closer to her work. You can't wait to see the place! She invites you over to tour the space when she gets settled, and you can't believe what you see. The place is absolutely huge. They've done so much remodeling and transformed the space into the perfect haven for her family. Everything is decorated so nicely, and the location of the house is stellar. You can tell that she's so excited and proud to show off the place, and you're just over-the-moon for her!

You get home and put your keys on the table by the front door and start to settle in for the night when suddenly your quaint and cozy house starts to feel a little...cramped. The rooms don't feel as spacious as they once did. Your neighbors are way too close and overbearing. You wish you had a bigger closet and more room for your shoe collection. And you start to resent your friend for her good fortune. Why does she need all that space anyway? You make a nice living too! Don't you deserve someplace nicer than this? JEALOUSY. It definitely isn't a good color on you, is it?

Has comparison ever forced jealousy into your heart? What was the result of this petty emotion?

Throughout the Bible, we find several harsh examples of what serious destruction jealousy can create. Possibly the best example of all is the story of Joseph and his brothers, so let's back up to the book of Genesis. Joseph's father favored Joseph out of his twelve sons and gave him a beautiful multicolored coat to wear. Joseph loved this coat and started to have prophetic dreams that he would rule over all his brothers. The dreams depicted twelve sheaves of grain in a field representing each brother. Eleven sheaves turned and bowed to Joseph's sheaf. Upon sharing these dreams with the eleven brothers, they became so jealous that they plotted to kill him. When they went to do the deed, they saw an opportunity to make some money and sold him into slavery instead and faked his death! (Genesis 37) Can you believe they did this to their own brother!? Jealousy can be so incredibly destructive once the enemy takes hold.

What other examples of jealousy can you find in the Bible?

____

____

____

____

This is definitely NOT what God wants for us. It's pretty plain in James 3:14–16 (ESV):

But if you have bitter jealousy and selfish ambition in your hearts, do not boast and be false to the truth. This is not the wisdom that comes down from above, but is earthly, unspiritual, demonic. For where jealousy and selfish ambition exist, there will be disorder and every vile practice.

For where jealousy and selfish ambition exist, there will be disorder and every vile practice.

James tells us outright that this isn't spiritual wisdom, it's earthly! It's a work of the flesh! Let that be our first clue! If the Bible says something is earthly, it means it's something formed by human beings and of the world, not from the Lord. It's of a sinful nature. For some reason, when someone has something we want, we think that we are automatically inferior. This couldn't be more false! "Good for her" doesn't mean "bad for you." It's just not your time, friend.

There's a phrase I like to say to myself when I'm feeling a little jealous: We have to share the sunshine! Looking back at our example, just because your friend has a great big, newly-renovated house doesn't mean your adorable, cozy place is any less special! A great way to debunk jealousy is to remind yourself that comparison is often the thief of joy.

Take a look at Romans 12:15. It has great advice for how to support one another despite your comparative differences. What does it say?

1. Illustrate or collage a multicolored coat in Genesis 37 and journal about ways that jealousy has disrupted your life like Joseph's brothers. Ask God to cast out that jealousy from your heart and replace it with love and support!

2. Focus on gratitude! Draw a house to represent your home and fill it with thanks to the Lord for all the blessings in your life.

DAY 4
Clay and Stone

When we're in a season of waiting, it's hard for us to stave off comparison. We feel like so much is out of our control that we start comparing our situations to others', hoping that what God has done for them, He will do for us. We grasp at the straws of comparison to find a hope and comfort for our waiting period. As I mentioned before, my husband and I waited over seven years to conceive a child, which, when you're in the middle of it, might as well be 1,000 years. My friends had pregnancy announcements popping up left and right. With social media, it was almost impossible for me to avoid them. Then came all the "bump" pictures they shared as their babies got bigger and their stomachs grew. I was surrounded by them. Friends my age who already had two children were getting pregnant again and lapping me. I kept thinking, "She's younger than me! Why does she get a baby and I don't? She already has two children; I don't even have one!" All I could do was pray and hope that my day was coming.

Are you in a season of waiting? What is it you're waiting for?

____

____

____

____

I threw myself into my work at the copy shop only to be offered my dream job at Illustrated Faith! Also at this point in time, we were living in a cute little apartment that was starting to feel too small. We knew that starting a family might not be in the cards for us, so we decided to look for a house to help fill that void. And we found one! Then my husband, Ian, left his awful job at a sporting goods store for a perfect one at a manufacturer with full benefits! Six months in, he was promoted! Then we got a spark in our hearts to try fertility treatments, and we were blessed with a baby on the very first cycle. It was incredible.

Looking back, I can literally see the stepping-stones the Lord was laying out for us. Little rocks in an everchanging river that we could use to get to the other side: Dream job. House. Ian's job. Promotion. Fertility treatments. Baby. I mean...WOW, GOD! All along He was making the perfect path for us, and we didn't even know it! All the waiting had a purpose: He was still preparing a place for us.

Can you see any stepping-stones the Lord has placed in your life? What markers can you see that are a part of His Master Plan?

God's plans are always better than ours. Always. But that's not always easy to see. Comparing our lives to someone else's is so pointless because they're not living your story—you are. Not all popcorn kernels pop at the same time. No one's story is going to track identically to yours! In the midst of the waiting, I reminded myself of Isaiah 64:8 (NIV®):

> ## YET YOU, LORD, ARE OUR FATHER. WE ARE THE CLAY,
> ## YOU ARE THE POTTER;
> ## WE ARE ALL THE WORK OF YOUR HAND.

I am the clay, and He is the potter. I repeated it in my head; I wrote it in my journal; I painted it in my art. I memorized it. I must allow the Master Artist to mold me and shape me as He sees fit. I'm not in charge here. The end result will be beautiful if I allow myself to be worked like clay and set on the right path. The same potter who shaped me is now molding the stepping-stones

for my journey. So whether you're waiting to graduate, waiting for a husband, an engagement, a baby, retirement, or just waiting for the light to turn green…He's working on it. *Wait for the LORD* (Psalm 27:14, NIV®)!

Write out a prayer to surrender yourself to the Lord. Prayerfully ask Him to mold you and shape you so that you may be ready and open to whatever comes next.

Creative Heart Check:

1. Use an image of a vase, pot, or bowl to symbolize your obedience and openness to the Lord's will.

2. Paint stepping-stones on your Bible or journal page and say a little prayer with each one to surrender your heart.

DAY 5
Humble Pie

In the throes of comparison, we often self-consciously see ourselves as the smaller piece of the puzzle. We feel insecure and inferior to our peers for whatever reason. From the outside looking in, we see the lives and accomplishments of others, and those accomplishments make us feel badly about our own lives. But every once in a while, we might find that our comparing has turned into judging others! This is sinful in a whole different way! We need to keep ourselves in check to make sure we're not having thoughts of superiority over those in our lives. Let me explain.

Everyone has that friend or sibling or cousin who's a hot mess. Maybe they're always late or messy beyond belief or chronically forgetful and disorganized. They just seem like their life needs a makeover. For me, that's my sister. If we have a family gathering or special event, we have to tell her it's a half hour earlier than it really is so that she'll arrive on time. The inside of her car looks like there's been a massive explosion. And she always shows up having forgotten something crucial or skipped some sort of responsibility. But gosh, do I love her! She's sunshine turned on full blast. Always happy, doesn't know a stranger, and up for anything. I'm the organized one and the one who makes fifty lists a day and the one who's always taken the lion's share of the responsibilities. So sometimes...sometimes she gets under my skin with her forgetfulness or carelessness.

Recently, we were getting together with family, and everyone was tasked with bringing something to pitch in for the meal. My sister's assignment was deviled eggs. She showed up fashionably late with, not deviled eggs, but a carton of raw eggs. Seriously!? She had forgotten to make them, so she brought the raw eggs along to hurry up and make before we ate. Oh boy.... So there are times when the way she lives her life really gets to me. Every time we have to wait on her because she's arrived late, I think to myself, "At least I'm not that disorganized," or "At least I've got my stuff together." But is that righteous? NO!

Let's look at the parable of the Pharisee and the Tax Collector. In this teachable story told by none other than Jesus Himself, we find a Pharisee and a tax collector praying in a temple:

> The Pharisee stood by himself and prayed: "God, I thank you that I am not like other people—robbers, evildoers, adulterers—or even like this tax collector. I fast twice a week and give a tenth of all I get." But the tax collector stood at a distance. He would not even look up to heaven, but beat his breast and said, "God, have mercy on me, a sinner." I tell you that this man, rather than the other, went home justified before God. For all those who exalt themselves will be humbled, and those who humble themselves will be exalted. (Luke 18:11–14, NIV®)

FOR ALL THOSE WHO EXALT THEMSELVES WILL BE HUMBLED, AND THOSE WHO HUMBLE THEMSELVES WILL BE EXALTED.

My inner monologue about being glad I'm not as disorganized as my sister is in the same vein as the Pharisee. God hears those thoughts and prayers. He hears my innermost exaltations of myself. See, the thing about my sister is that even when she's having an especially tragic day being a mess, she's always apologetic and humble. She comes through the door already apologizing for making us wait or for not having the right kind of eggs. (Ha!) In that way, she's humble and cognizant of her shortcomings, just like the tax collector. I, on the other hand, might have some real work to do with humility. Those types of thoughts of superiority are very judging, and that's not mine to do. We're playing the comparison game, but from the other side of the fence. And no side is a winner in that game.

So I'm asking you right now to humble yourself. We can see how destructive and damaging comparison can be. Don't let these thoughts that put yourself on a pedestal creep in. Truly, we must give each other grace, even if it's undeserved. We are all sinners and fall short of the glory of God. We are all so undeserving of His love and grace, but we receive it anyway! Don't give in to boasting or exalting yourself. Instead, eat a big, huge slice of humble pie.

Stop right now and write out a prayer asking the Lord to humble you. Not only about your own actions but ask Him to open your heart to the actions of others and allow grace to flood your being.

Creative Heart Check:

1. Design your own juicy piece of humble pie and accompany it with a prayer of humility. Ask the Lord for grace in your thoughts and actions.

2. Create space to journal a special tribute to someone in your life who exhibits humility and grace to others. Journal about how you can adopt some of their behaviors in your faith walk.

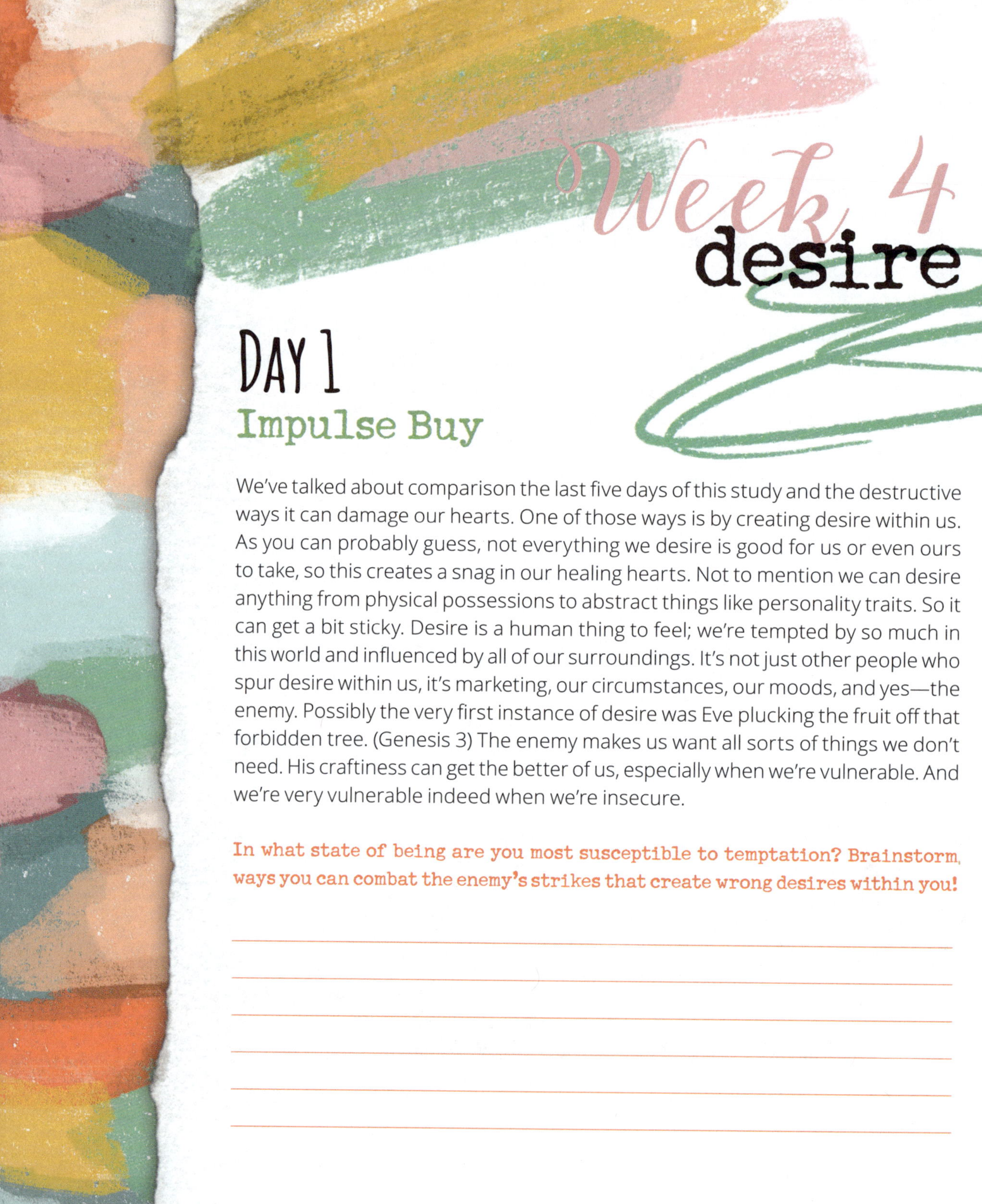

Day 1
Impulse Buy

We've talked about comparison the last five days of this study and the destructive ways it can damage our hearts. One of those ways is by creating desire within us. As you can probably guess, not everything we desire is good for us or even ours to take, so this creates a snag in our healing hearts. Not to mention we can desire anything from physical possessions to abstract things like personality traits. So it can get a bit sticky. Desire is a human thing to feel; we're tempted by so much in this world and influenced by all of our surroundings. It's not just other people who spur desire within us, it's marketing, our circumstances, our moods, and yes—the enemy. Possibly the very first instance of desire was Eve plucking the fruit off that forbidden tree. (Genesis 3) The enemy makes us want all sorts of things we don't need. His craftiness can get the better of us, especially when we're vulnerable. And we're very vulnerable indeed when we're insecure.

In what state of being are you most susceptible to temptation? Brainstorm ways you can combat the enemy's strikes that create wrong desires within you!

I know I'm extremely prone to wanting what I don't need when I'm unhappy. My first instinct is to look around and make a plan for how to fix my negative emotions. Some people call that plan retail therapy. Often I feel a hole in my life, and my solution is to shove a shopping bag in that hole. Come to think of it, I do that when I'm happy too. Shopping makes me happy. And the thing is, I wouldn't even call myself materialistic! The things that matter most to me are my family and friends—I could take or leave everything else. Well, maybe a few art supplies wouldn't hurt! *Wink* I'll confess that during the COVID-19 quarantine, when we were all so on edge and unsure, I had an online shopping problem. I bought new couch pillows, a ridiculous watch, and a teeth whitening kit. I probably could have lived without all those things I bought on impulse, but it was my way of coping. I used shopping to fill the cracks of my unhappiness.

What's a purchase that you made impulsively to fill a hole in your life?

My husband and I are currently in the market for an exercise bike—one that we can have in the house and use for fitness even when it's raining or snowing. The real origin of us suddenly wanting an exercise bike, though, is that I felt insecure about my body and thought up a purchase that might patch the hole I was feeling inside. Now some might say an exercise bike is a healthy purchase that will improve our overall health and wellness. That's true, but without one key component, that effort is useless. I'm talking about gratitude.

Gratitude is the key to combatting so many yucky feelings that plague us. If you fill your heart with gratitude, there's less room for insecurity, unhealthy desire, unhappiness, and misery. Gratitude breeds joy. Thanking the Lord heartily for what we have (instead of lamenting what we don't have) is like a tonic we can drink to heal those cracks. So in my situation, instead of my knee-jerk reaction to shop to make myself feel better, I should have tried thanking the Lord sincerely for the body He has given me. I should have voiced my gratitude for my health and thanked Him for making me in His image and giving me a vessel in which to live for His will. It makes a world of difference to stop and ponder the wonders in your life and count the blessings instead of automatically wanting more.

Read Psalm 103:2–5. Just based on this passage, what things can you thank God for with elation and gratitude? Use your own words in the form of a prayer.

"Rejoice always." That's a command given more than once in the Bible in different ways. You might remember, *Count it all joy* (James 1:2), for example. In 1 Thessalonians, the Bible specifically says,

> **REJOICE ALWAYS, PRAY CONTINUALLY, GIVE THANKS IN ALL CIRCUMSTANCES.**
>
> 1 THESSALONIANS 5:16–18 (NIV®)

God wants us to come to Him first when we're feeling vulnerable. Otherwise, your next impulse buy might be a robotic toaster or a genuine llama. (You can buy anything on the internet!) So go with the Bible's not-so-secret advice: Start with fervent gratitude, then go from there.

Creative Heart Check:

1. Create a "shopping list," but instead of things to buy, make it things to thank the Lord for! Top it off with an image of a delivery box or shopping bag!

2. Incorporate the image of an apple to illustrate the first act of desire. Then write about what desires are on your heart. Ask the Lord to take them and replace them with gratitude!

DAY 2

One More Bite

Last night I sat down with my husband to watch TV and ate two slices of apple pie. The first slice was just so good, and I couldn't resist a second helping. Slightly crunchy apples, sweet gooey filling, and savory crust. I topped it off with a big glass of cold milk. Mmmmm...my mouth is watering just thinking about it. I felt so satisfied afterward. But then a little later I paid for it. I had a stomachache, and it was clear that I had overdone it. Not to mention my blood sugar was probably through the roof. What's that saying? My eyes were bigger than my stomach? Sometimes we make choices that aren't good for us. It should have been obvious that I shouldn't eat two slices of pie, but the temptation trumped the facts. It happens to all of us.

James 1:14 (ESV) says, *But each person is tempted when he is lured and enticed by his own desire.* Desire can be a dangerous thing! Sometimes it leads us to make bad or unhealthy choices for ourselves. We think we know what we want or need, so we follow through.

Name a small instance where your desire got the best of you and you made a poor choice. How about a bigger, more important instance?

____

____

____

____

Truthfully though, only God knows what desires will benefit us in the long run. Some things might seem sweet at the time, but the satisfaction is short-lived, and we're left feeling unhappy. (Like two hearty helpings of apple pie!) This principle can really apply to anything in our lives: possessions, the foods we eat, or even relationships. There are times we want to make a relationship or friendship work so bad, but the results are

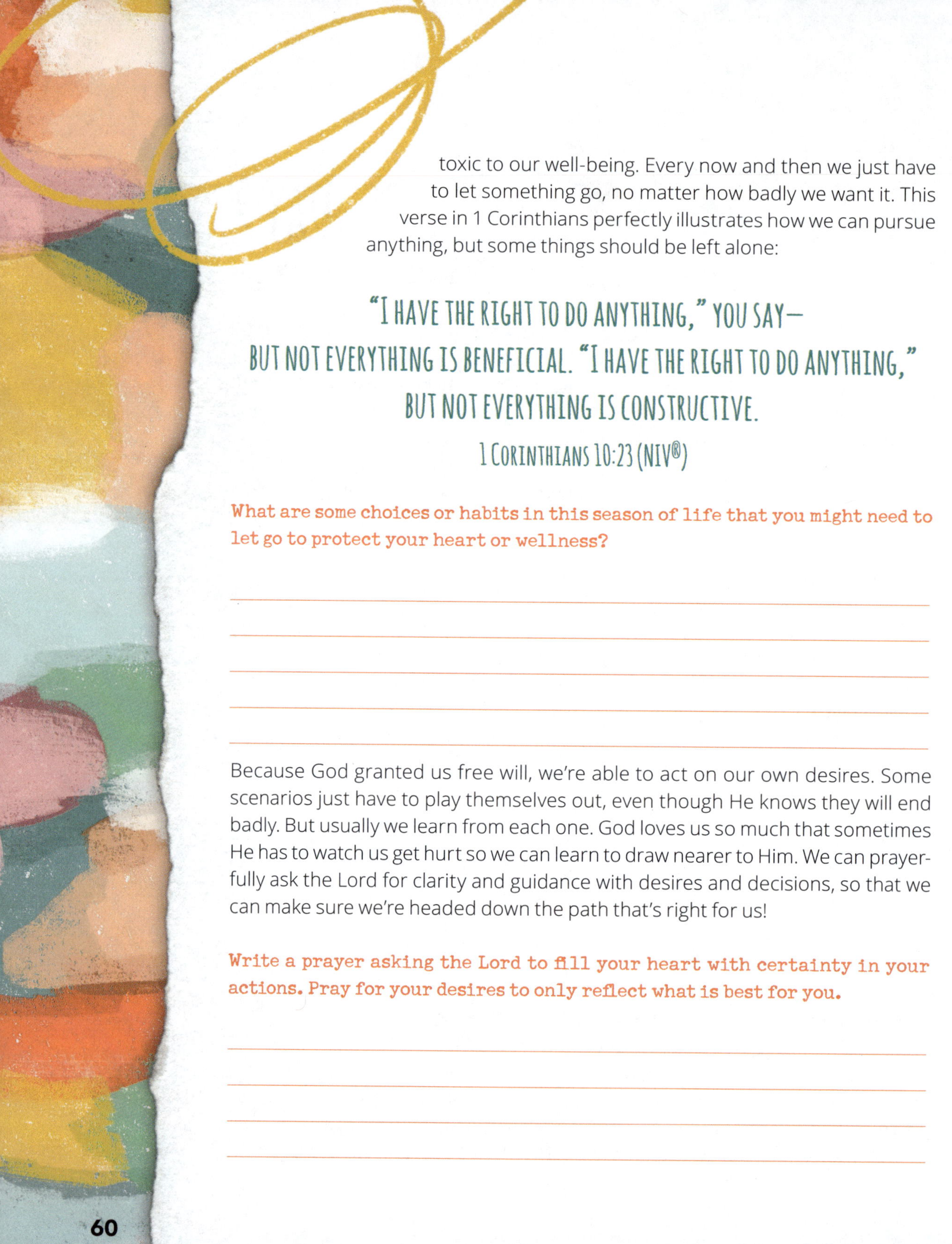

toxic to our well-being. Every now and then we just have to let something go, no matter how badly we want it. This verse in 1 Corinthians perfectly illustrates how we can pursue anything, but some things should be left alone:

"I HAVE THE RIGHT TO DO ANYTHING," YOU SAY—
BUT NOT EVERYTHING IS BENEFICIAL. "I HAVE THE RIGHT TO DO ANYTHING,"
BUT NOT EVERYTHING IS CONSTRUCTIVE.

1 Corinthians 10:23 (NIV®)

What are some choices or habits in this season of life that you might need to let go to protect your heart or wellness?

____

____

____

____

____

Because God granted us free will, we're able to act on our own desires. Some scenarios just have to play themselves out, even though He knows they will end badly. But usually we learn from each one. God loves us so much that sometimes He has to watch us get hurt so we can learn to draw nearer to Him. We can prayerfully ask the Lord for clarity and guidance with desires and decisions, so that we can make sure we're headed down the path that's right for us!

Write a prayer asking the Lord to fill your heart with certainty in your actions. Pray for your desires to only reflect what is best for you.

____

____

____

____

Creative Heart Check:

1. Use images of junk food to represent poor choices you may be making in your life. Pray that the Lord will replace them with righteous actions and personal wellness!

2. Illustrate a map with a fork in the road. Which way will you take to live your best life?

DAY 3

Genies and Gumball Machines

I kept a journal every day of my four years of high school. I still have the volumes of journals I wrote tucked away in our attic space. If you were to crack open the colorful covers, you would find a cross section of my life at the time: thoughts, feelings, dreams, musings about boyfriends, pro and con lists, notes passed back and forth, and collages. You would know that I had dreams of traveling and moving out of my small hometown. I wanted to go to Europe and create art in the parks just like Claude Monet. I had big aspirations of living there unattached to anything: FREE. But God, as He often does, had other plans for me.

I met Ian in college and fell fast in love. All of our friends were Film and Television Studies majors like Ian, and they were all bound for Burbank, California, to pursue the film industry while we were looking for an apartment here in Indiana to start a family. We wanted good careers, a nice place to live, and a way to build our family up piece by piece. We wanted more time together and

less time working demanding jobs. You might think we felt like we were being left behind, but we didn't. Because through prayer, the Lord had given us a new path. Instead of setting off for worlds unknown, we were settling down.

What plans has God replaced in your life through prayer and a surrendered heart?

____

____

____

____

You have probably heard this verse quoted at least a few times:

> ## DELIGHT YOURSELF IN THE LORD, AND HE WILL GIVE YOU THE DESIRES OF YOUR HEART.
>
> PSALM 37:4 (ESV)

But this passage is often misunderstood. It makes God sound like a magic genie. He's going to come out of a golden lamp and grant you three wishes! Whatever you desire will be yours!… Nope. That's not really how it works. What this scripture actually means is that through prayer, the Lord will place inside you the desires that He wants for you. He literally gives you the desires of your heart that are best. When I learned this tidbit from a sermon at church, it

blew my mind. Kaboom! We can surrender to God with an open heart and ask Him to put dreams inside us that align with His will! He's not a gumball machine—you don't put in a quarter and get exactly what you want. He will instill in you the desires aligned with what He seeks for you.

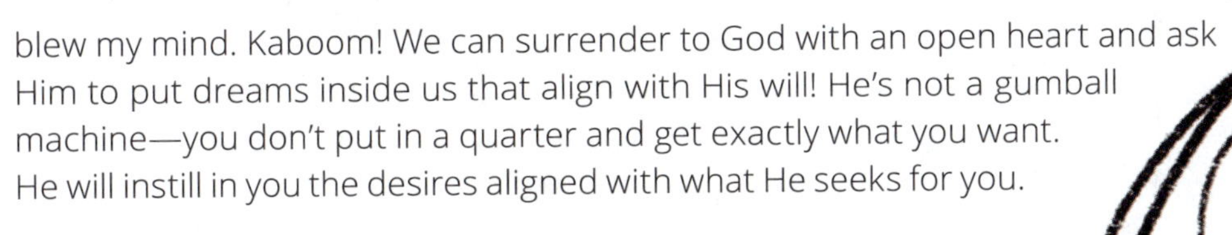

Read Proverbs 3:5–6. What does this verse and Psalm 37:4 have in common?

____

____

____

Because of this beautiful practice, God gave Ian and me the desires and dreams of a family. When all our friends were leaving us behind, we were perfectly content with our new path because it wasn't just what we wanted, it's what our Father wanted for us as well. I often think about what life would have been like if we hadn't settled down. We never would have walked the stepping-stones He set up for us, and my testimony would look drastically different. Who knows exactly what life would be like, but I know it would be a full 180 degrees from what it is now. I still like to think about what's in my journals: traveling and taking a lap around Europe. I think there's still time to do some of those things; we'll just have to see what the Lord has in store for the next chapter of our lives. He makes our paths straight! (Proverbs 3:5–6)

Creative Heart Check:

1. Collage a separate piece of paper with dreams, prayers, and aspirations. Mix them with paint and other mediums. Then cut a heart from that paper and use it in your Bible.

2. God is not a gumball machine! Use an image of one to remind yourself to remain open to what comes next.

DAY 4
Finding Joy

I'm a work-from-home mama. (Picture me showing off my strong arms, muscleman style!) It's definitely not easy. There are days when I get nothing productive done all day simply because I'm chasing around a little squirmy toddler named Quinn. He needs my help with everything he does and gets into everything. He needs a sippy cup filled? I'm the girl for the job. He crunches crackers into the living room carpet? I'm the one who sweeps it up. Quinn can't find his favorite stuffed owl? I know exactly where he left it. So each day has very abbreviated work time. (If you count trying to type an email while dodging him banging on the keyboard as "work time.") Oftentimes I find myself working at night while he sleeps, which takes away from my relaxing and decompressing time.

Toward the end of last year, I started to lose my spark for our daytime routine. I was overworked, run down, disorganized, and frustrated. I needed more hours in the day. Don't get me wrong—I desperately wanted to stay home with Quinn and didn't want to send him to a daycare. I know being in his own environment is what is best for him, but I had misplaced my joy for the work-from-home lifestyle. I was telling myself that this was just how it was going to be if I continued to stay home with him. But I had to reevaluate my priorities and ask myself: "What does God want for me?"

Have you ever struggled to find joy in your everyday routine? God wants us to find the blessings in even the most mundane tasks. Take some time to check in with the Father about your everyday life and ask Him what He wants for you.

If you've never considered or prayed about what God wants for you, it's a real eye-opener. I always picture those Venn diagrams we had to use in school. Two overlapping circles. On the right, what I want. On the left, what God wants. And the part where it overlaps in the middle is where joy is found. Wouldn't it be nice if those circles overlapped completely? If we only desired exactly what our Heavenly Father wants for us? But that's usually not the case. When I was struggling, I considered how God wanted me to feel as a mother and as a person in this season in my life. I prayed, and the answer I got was to consider the fruit of the Spirit.

The fruit of the Spirit (Galatians 5:22–23) is a brilliant place to start when you're asking yourself what God wants for you. Love, joy, peace, patience, kindness, goodness, faithfulness, gentleness, and self-control are all things the Lord wants to see in our lives and through our actions.

We each have our own spiritual gifts. Which of the fruit of the Spirit come easily to you, and which ones do you have to work for? What do we gain by pursuing the fruit of the Spirit?

I LOVE my son, but I needed JOY in our daytime routine. I needed PEACE about how Quinn was being cared for. I needed to create a way for me to have more PATIENCE with him and more KINDNESS for my husband at night. The answer was to bring in a part-time nanny to watch him a few hours a day, so I could get back to regular work hours. It was going to cost us money, but the dividends we would get in joy would be immeasurable.

After we found a nanny to come watch Quinn during the week, the circles on my Venn diagram were starting to align more and more. I got my spark back, and the GOODNESS it infused in our home has been off the charts. God really knows what is best for me, and He knows what's best for you too. FAITHFULNESS is priceless, and prayer will lead you to a better understanding of what God wants for you. Knowing the difference is half the battle if we have the SELF-CONTROL to resist

what we desire and not forsake the Lord's presence! So please humbly draw near to the Father and ask Him to reveal what He wants for you and to fill you with the the fruit of the Spirit. It's more satisfying than you could ever imagine!

Creative Heart Check:

1. Illustrate some fruit to represent the fruit of the Spirit, and write down ways you can exhibit each fruit in your life.

2. Draw your own Venn diagram and fill out what you want and what you feel God wants for you.

Day 5
Not Our Home

All this talk about desire has probably made you really consider what it is you want. I hope you've been prayerfully consulting with the Lord on this one. Unfortunately, when we ask God for something, He doesn't always say yes. Sometimes it's a resounding no, which probably isn't what we want to hear at the time. Hopefully, we come to terms with God's answer and realize He is closing a door because He has something equally beautiful for us in store. We don't always have to walk through the door to be blessed in abundance. Beauty and wonder are found on this side of the door too.

When was the last time God said no to your prayers and questions? Consider how He might have been saving you for something better.

____

____

____

____

For months our family had been praying that we wouldn't have to cancel our vacation to Florida. We were really looking forward to heading south for the sunny weather and lying on the beach while the kids played in the sand. It was going to be such a sweet time of sight-seeing and relaxation away from our everyday lives. But unfortunately, the answer we received from the Lord was no. To date, this pandemic rages on, and the virus, among other reasons, is preventing us from making the trip. But another answer I felt the Lord conveying to me is that vacations, like many of the other things we ask God for, are of this world, not from God. In 1 John 2:15–17, we're told not to love the things of this world, for when we do, we're not focused on the love of the Father. I considered this and wondered what parts of that vacation would be from the Lord. Togetherness and love are the bits that we receive from Him, and we can certainly be together and love each other right here in Indiana. We don't have to take an expensive trip to access the love of our family and the love of our Father. Worshipping that vacation is not the way to the Lord, but coming together in fellowship definitely is.

Are you in pursuit of something of this world? How can you amend your prayers so that they're more in line with godly pursuits?

Anything of this world is transient and temporary. This is not our home (Hebrews 13:14); we're just passing through life on earth on our way to our eternal home with the Lord. It took me a long time to fully embrace this idea because, truthfully, I love my life. But the biblical truth that this life isn't the end game really puts into perspective that the things we seek might not be righteous. Seeking desires of the flesh won't serve us; only seeking Jesus will do that.

When I'm feeling greedy in my desires, I like to recall Hebrews 13:5. It's an in-your-face passage with specific orders to appreciate what we have.

Copy down Hebrews 13:5, and underline or highlight the main points of the passage.

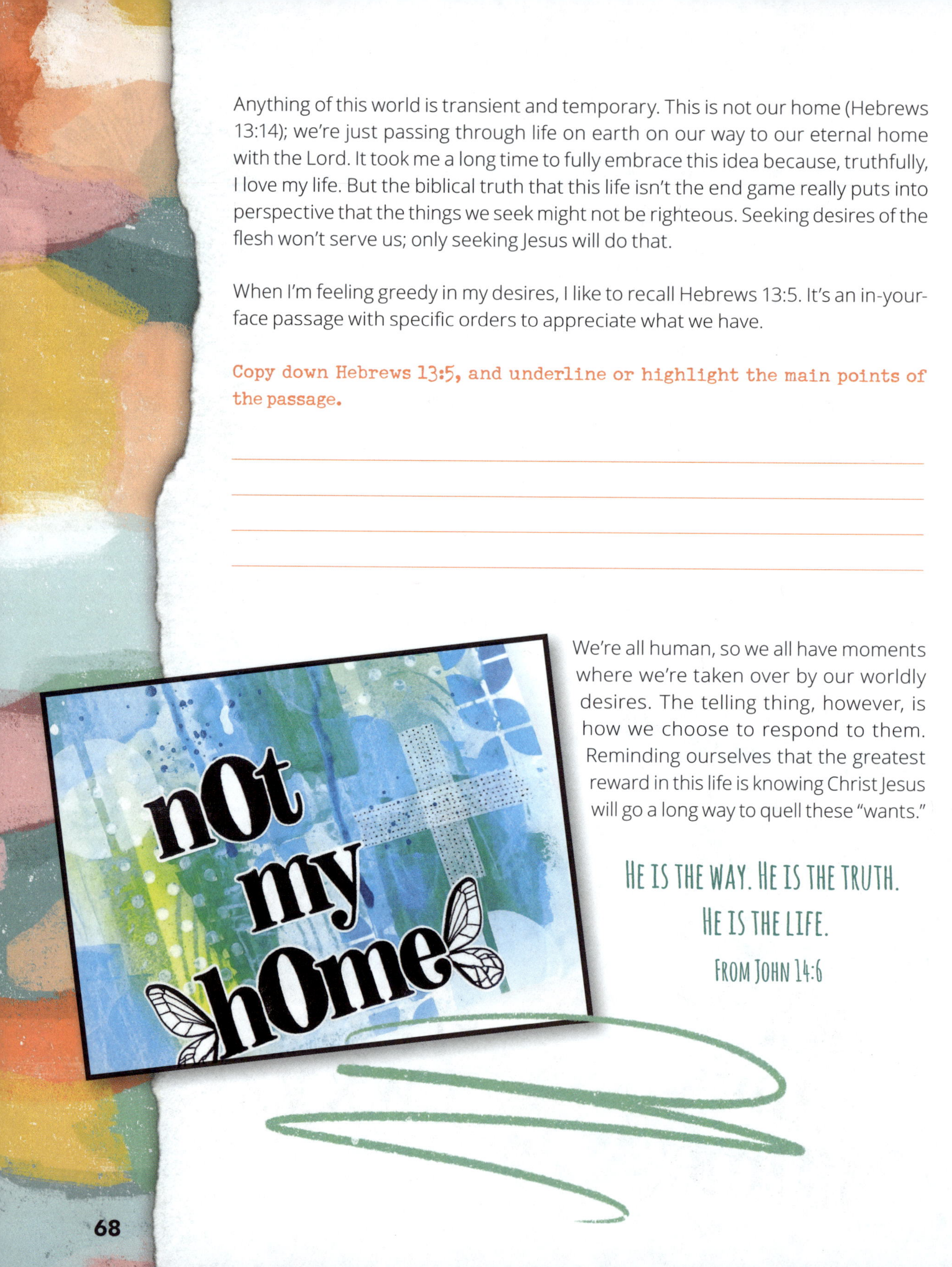

We're all human, so we all have moments where we're taken over by our worldly desires. The telling thing, however, is how we choose to respond to them. Reminding ourselves that the greatest reward in this life is knowing Christ Jesus will go a long way to quell these "wants."

HE IS THE WAY. HE IS THE TRUTH. HE IS THE LIFE.

FROM JOHN 14:6

1. Create a globe on your Bible page and title it with "This is not my home." It's a great reminder that we are not of this world!

2. Write down some worldly pursuits, then paint over them. Everything in this world is temporary, especially desires of the flesh.

Closing Prayer

Lord, as we close the book for this study, I pray that we have all grown a little closer to You. You soak us in Your profound goodness and love each and every day, and I pray that we don't take it for granted. Please help our hearts to remain open to whatever comes next, whether it be trouble or triumph. Knowing You has given us the tools to face whatever comes our way because Your presence goes before us. Thank You for giving us a creative spirit and for the ability to use it to bring all the glory back to You. And thank You for giving us each other. A cord of three strands is not easily broken, and we really are stronger together in fellowship. In Your precious name I pray, Amen.

Leader's Guide

Dear Leader,

Saying I'm thrilled that you chose *Messy Art, Full Heart* to work through with your group is a vast understatement! It feels surreal to be addressing you this way! I've been praying for you throughout this entire process, so just know that you're entering a precious space of being equipped to lead others. God led you to this study, and He will hold your hand through it as well, even through the tough questions and discussions!

In the Leader's Guide, I outline my suggestions to prompt discussion and ways to experiment creatively. The key to working through these challenging topics is to keep the discussion open so that your group members can participate with open, honest, and surrendered hearts. In addition to my suggestions, please listen to the Holy Spirit as you lead and take the conversation where the Lord nudges it. Each person has had different experiences, and the questions will resonate differently within each heart.

Don't feel intimidated to lead your group creatively! Your enthusiasm and passion for Scripture are what will feed your members' hearts the most. God has uniquely qualified you to share your creative spirit. This is a part of your testimony—share it!

Thank you again for reaching for *Messy Art, Full Heart* to work through with your group! Thank you for allowing me to play a tiny part in the heart work you are doing, wherever you are.

With love,

Elaine Davis

P.S. If you ever need to contact me, you can find me on Instagram at @mrs.elaine.davis or via email at kelainedavis@gmail.com.

Before You Begin

Pose a few questions for your group members to think about in the time leading up to the start of your study:

- What calls you to this group? What made you interested in joining?

- What mediums might you want to use in the creative portion of the study?

- What challenges are you facing in your life that you might want to work through personally?

- What goals do you have for working through this study?

Send out a short supply list of things each person might want to bring with them to complete the devotional and creative part of the study. Here are my suggestions:

- Ink pen and pencil

- Paper for notes

- A journaling Bible or art journal

- Scissors

- Paint brushes

- Glue stick and/or adhesive tape runner

- Alphabet stickers

- Stamps

- Stamping block

- Ink pad

- Also remind your group members to print out their book printable before coming to class!

- Cheap craft paints
- Cheap makeup sponges
- Paper plates (for palettes)
- Stencils
- Colored pencils and/or markers
- Tissue paper
- White card stock
- Old magazines (to cut from)
- A stapler
- A heat gun
- Washi tape

Suggested Meeting Itinerary

I thought I would share the basic itinerary flow I use when I host meet-ups or workshops! This is a simple formula you can follow for your own meetings, but it might need to be adjusted based on your time allotment or overall feel of the group. Make it your own!

5 min ....Opening Prayer

10 min ....Introductions/Icebreaker
(if this is your first meeting together)

30-45 min....Read that day's devo/scriptures and discuss

10 min..........Demonstrate a technique or product
(or have a group member demonstrate)

1 hour ....Creative work free time

15 min ....Show and Tell

5 min ....Closing Prayer

Book Outline and Companion Material

DAY 1
Natural Light

Theme: Faith conquers worry and doubt.

Ask: What do you think it was like for the Israelites being led out of Egypt by a pillar of fire? How can that feel similar to our own situations?

Demo: Offer examples of your own Bible pages to show your group members how they can spread paint on a page.

DAY 2
Bible Bookworm

Theme: Everyone worries, even those believed to be the most devout Christians.

Ask: Why do you think we subconsciously fight the Word of God telling us not to be anxious? What forces in our lives are trumping His words?

Demo: Show the group what a tip-in is. (It's a paper or card attached into the pages that can be flipped open like a book.) Demo how to attach it with washi tape on one side.

Day 3

Fixer-Upper

Theme: Worry isn't a good teacher; seek wise counsel.

Ask: How do you feel about your abilities when you need to ask for advice or help? How can we reverse negative thinking and remember that the Lord wants us to ask for advice from others when we need it?

Demo: Share different ways to create a bold title on your Bible page: paint, stickers, stamps, etc. What other ways can you think of?

Day 4

Little and Loved

Theme: There is no worry too small for God.

Ask: Have the group share examples of how the Lord has provided for them in big or small ways in the past. How does this support the claim that He will provide for us no matter what the situation?

Demo: Create an abstract scribbly background with children's crayons, art crayons, or other medium to demonstrate ways to embrace "child-like art."

Day 5

Perfect Power

Theme: We are weak and we need to rely fully on Him.

Ask: As women, we often respond to situations of weakness and stress by trying to manage and control the outcome. What are some tactics we can use to take a step back and allow God to do His work?

Demo: Try your hand at "blind contouring." This technique is drawing something while blindfolded without lifting your pen or marker. This is a great technique to mimic surrendering in the moment and allowing God to work in you! It also creates some gorgeous abstract art!

Week 2
fear

DAY 1

Name It and Claim It

Theme: Establishing your fears can help you fight them.

Ask: How does it make you feel that God knows the outcome of our situation before we've even encountered it? How does that affect your willingness to surrender to Him?

Demo: Create envelopes out of cute patterned paper by taking apart a regular envelope and tracing it.

DAY 2

Fight or Flight

Theme: Running away from our problems doesn't serve us.

Ask: Have you ever tried to run away from fear and God told you to turn around and go back? If yes, what was the circumstance?

Demo: Teach the class how to collage using watered-down liquid glue and a paint brush.

Day 3

Heart Work

Theme: God will show up for us amidst our fears.

Ask: Discuss ways you can carve out specific time to pray. Example: Maybe it's while you're on the treadmill, while you wash dishes, or on your commute to work.

Demo: Try stamping with non-traditional items mounted on a wood block. A few ideas are fun foam, yarn, leaves, bits of canvas, or milk jug lids.

Day 4

First Aid

Theme: Whom shall we fear?

Ask: Discuss your reactions to Isaiah 55:8–9. How does the group respond to the claim that "our fear implies that we aren't confident in the Lord's abilities and might"?

Demo: Get some gold leaf flakes at your craft store and experiment with different adhesives.

Day 5

Suit Up

Theme: Don't let your shield of faith drop!

Ask: Describe some ways we use the armor of God in our everyday lives.

Demo: Make photocopies of a blank shield shape for people to cut out and decorate. It's fun to imagine our armor of God in bright colors and patterns!

week 3
comparison

Day 1

Click of Approval

Theme: Don't compare your own life to someone's social media feed.

Ask: What are some other forms of media that give us unrealistic and false representations of what our real lives should look like? How should we respond?

Demo: If you haven't already, demonstrate how to incorporate printables into your work. Feel free to show the printable printed on different types of paper. (Example: card stock, copy paper, clear sticker paper, etc.)

Day 2

Shame Spiral

Theme: We don't need anyone's approval but the Lord's.

Ask: Would you ever walk up to someone you loved (or even someone you DON'T love!) and tell them that their artwork was ugly? When we are ashamed and critical of ourselves, we're criticizing His handiwork!

Demo: Gather some alpha stamp sets and give a demo on mixed alpha titles! Mixing up the letter styles is a great way to add interest to titles or journaling!

Day 3

Share the Sunshine

Theme: Jealousy isn't righteous.

Ask: Think of a time when jealousy entered your heart. How did it affect your state of mind? Did you feel convicted?

Demo: Bring scraps of tissue paper and collage them onto a piece of white card stock. Then cut shapes out of the collage to use in your Bible!

Day 4

Clay and Stone

Theme: God's plan is always better than ours.

Ask: What examples from the Bible can we identify where people were waiting, slowly being shaped by the Master Potter? Why is the clay and potter the perfect metaphor for our relationship with the Lord?

Demo: Tie bits of ribbon and trim to paperclips to create a stylish way you can mark your own stepping-stones in your Bible.

Day 5

Humble Pie

Theme: We should avoid self-exalted thinking!

Ask: Think about the thoughts you've had in the past couple of days. Was there any self-exalted thinking? Are those the kinds of thoughts you want the Father to have heard? How can you redirect your thinking toward grace?

Demo: Bring personal photos of people who can be models of humility for you. Try layering them up with patterned paper, doilies, and other little bits to bring emphasis to the person in the photo.

Week 4
desire

DAY 1

Impulse Buy

Theme: Gratitude breeds contentment.

Ask: Discuss the idea of "count it all joy" from James 1:2. Why does James ask us to count it all joy, even when we don't feel joyful?

Demo: Demonstrate stamping with an apple to represent Eve eating from the forbidden tree. Slice an apple in half from top to bottom, then dip the apple half in paint and stamp it on your Bible page! Good childlike fun!

DAY 2

One More Bite

Theme: Sometimes we desire things that aren't good for us.

Ask: How do you feel after you know you've made a bad choice? Never forget that no one is too far gone for God to use! He will definitely use that instance for good and bring you closer to Him in the end.

Demo: One of my favorite ways to Bible Journal is by using non-traditional supplies! Save the packaging or labels from some junk food that your group members can use on their pages to represent bad choices. The results can be very cool!

Day 3

Genies and Gumball Machines

Theme: He will give you the desires of your heart through prayer.

Ask: How might your life circumstances be different if it wasn't for the Lord guiding your desires?

Demo: Paint with bubble wrap! Grab some bubble wrap, dip the bubbles in paint, and smash it on your pages for a cool mixed media effect.

Day 4

Finding Joy

Theme: What we want vs. what God wants for us.

Ask: Zero in on which Fruit of the Spirit you think you need to work on the most. What are some examples of other things God wants for our lives aside from the Fruit of the Spirit?

Demo: Experiment with different ways to apply paint. Some of my favorites are using a baby wipe, credit card, or a comb for a fun texture.

Day 5

Not Our Home

Theme: This world is not our home.

Ask: Discuss earthly desires that might hold us back from experiencing full and complete love for the Father. How can we remind ourselves that certain pleasures exist only in this home, not the next?

Demo: Work with the class to create 3x4 cards to trade and/or give away. Make them tiny works of art and then pass them on to others. This can represent that things in our lives are only temporary.

Acknowledgements

Messy Art, Full Heart came together with the talents and hearts of many, many people. First I want to thank everyone at Warner Christian Resources for the incredible opportunity to share this book with the world. When they approached me to write for them, I kept pinching myself because I was sure I was dreaming. WCR has been nothing but wonderful to me throughout this entire process. Specifically, I owe so much gratitude to Julie Campbell, my editor, for holding my hand through my first publishing experience and for being such a great cheerleader. She continues, to this day, to be such a source of wise counsel and encouragement. Not to mention she's the most wonderful friend!

I would like to acknowledge Ranger Ink for allowing me to showcase their products throughout these pages. I couldn't have completed the art projects without the use of their range of ink colors, sprays, stencils, and tools. As an artist, I find their products indispensable.

Crossway is another brand without which I couldn't have completed this project. My favorite Bibles are from Crossway, and I would have been lost without their permission to show them in *Messy Art, Full Heart*.

I also have to give a shout out to my dear friend Winter Lawson of Four Seasons Photography for photographing my head shots for the book. She did an amazing job, even though I'm completely awkward in front of the camera, haha!

Illustrated Faith has obviously played a huge role in bringing about this book. Thank you to IF for allowing me to use so many of your products in my projects: die cuts, washi tape, and everything in between. And a specific, personal thank you to Shanna Noel. She is the best boss, sounding board, source of wisdom and inspiration, cheerleader, and close friend a girl could ask for. I want to thank her for giving me a chance over five years ago and bringing me along on the Illustrated Faith journey. I've gained so much exposure, experience, and opportunities since joining the IF staff. Thank you, Shanna, for helping me get to this point. I owe so much to you!

And now a group of people who have held me up my whole life: my family. Thank you to Nana and Papaw for always believing I would write a book someday. They have been saying this since I was in grade school, so I thank them for their love and belief in my abilities. Thank you to my in-laws, Matt, Renée, Riley, and Eric, for their input and support surrounding this project. Thank you to my sister, Anna, for always cheering me on, no matter what the situation is! I can always count on her to be excited for me each step of the way. Thank you to my mom and dad for the consistent strength, support, and pep talks. Whenever I'm doubting myself, they remind me who I am and where I come from—a family that loves big and doesn't quit.

My husband, Ian, is by far my biggest supporter and I'm his. There have been multiple times throughout this process where I've broken down crying, and he's always the one to put the pieces back together. His superpower is knowing just what to say to me in all circumstances. Thanks doesn't quite seem like enough. I love you, babe! Plus I can't forget little Quinn! Big thanks to him for being my inspiration for several of these devotions and for all the squishy hugs that power my personal energy bank.

The biggest thanks of all to the Lord for allowing me this amazing, incredible opportunity to share my heart and testimony with so many. Thank You for all the stepping-stones You set up in my life to get me to this point. You are so, so good.

Exclusive Printables

The following artwork was created exclusively for this study by Elaine Davis, author of *Messy Art, Full Heart*. For each week of the study, Elaine has included a full page of corresponding printables that you can use in your journaling Bible, your art journal, or however your heart desires! We simply ask that you use this link for your own private use, as it is a bonus for those who purchase the book only. Download the printable pages in 8 ½ x 11 format as many times as you'd like at www.warnerpress.org/messy-art-download.

Enjoy your free printables, and feel free to tag @WarnerChristianResources on social media when you share your journaling! We'd love to see what you create!

His grace is sufficient.
no worry too small.
He says do not be anxious about anything
anxiety do not be anxious
overcome with worry faith
in Him light drives out
darkness seek advice wise
counsel surround yourself
with love and support God
childlike faith my worries
give it to God prayer & plea
no worry too small He cares
for me His power is perfect

name it & claim it
LOVE
fear
do not be afraid &
peace within you fearless
name it & claim it nail it
to the cross fight or flight
heart work God moment stand
firm solid as a rock Jesus
I put on The Armor of God
Shield of Faith carry me
line of defense be courageous
whom shall I fear? strength

Messy Art, Full Heart
Chapter 3: Comparison
BEAUTIFUL
crowned
!!!
???
comparison social media &
shame spiral do not feel
ashamed God's approval I am
righteous share the sunshine
beautiful jealousy spiritual
wisdom heart check waiting
we are the clay God's timing
blessings stepping stones
surrender insecure & inferior
humility I feel seen loved

desire impulse buy gratitude

forbidden fruit Adam & Eve

what I want vs. what He wants

guard your heart

God isn't a gumball machine

desires of my heart finding

joy Fruit of the Spirit love

this is not our home heaven

& unanswered prayers things

of this world Jesus is life

Notes